S0-ARL-765

SURFCRAFT

Design and the
Culture of Board Riding

SURF CRAFT

Design and the
Culture of Board Riding

Richard Kenvin
Edited by Christine Knoke
Photographs by Ryan Field

MINGEI INTERNATIONAL MUSEUM, SAN DIEGO
MIT PRESS, CAMBRIDGE, MA, AND LONDON

This book is published in conjunction with the exhibition *Surf Craft: Design and the Culture of Board Riding*, presented at Mingei International Museum from June 21, 2014, to January 11, 2015.

Mingei International Museum
1439 El Prado
San Diego, CA 92101
www.mingei.org

Funding was provided by the Myron Eichen Memorial Fund at The San Diego Foundation, Ken and Sandy High, and UBS Financial Services.

Copyright © 2014
All rights reserved. No part of this publication may be reproduced or transmitted in any form or by any means, electronic or mechanical, including photocopy, recording, or any information storage or retrieval system, without permission in writing from the publisher.

Library of Congress Cataloging-in-Publication Data

Kenvin, Richard.
 Surf craft : design and the culture of board riding / Richard Kenvin ; edited by Christine Knoke ; photographs by Ryan Field, Mingei International Museum, San Diego.
   pages cm
 Includes bibliographical references.
 ISBN 978-0-262-02760-1 (alk. paper)
1. Surfboards--United States--Design and construction--History. 2. Surfing--United States. 3. Surfing--Social aspects--United States. 4. Subculture. I. Title.
 GV839.6.K48 2014
 797.3'2--dc23
                                    2014017714

10 9 8 7 6 5

Published by Mingei International Museum in association with The MIT Press.

Distributed by The MIT Press
One Rogers Street
Cambridge, MA 02142
www.mitpress.mit.edu

MIT Press books may be purchased at special quantity discounts for business or sales promotional use. For information, please contact special_sales@mitpress.mit.edu.

Produced by Lucia|Marquand, Seattle
www.luciamarquand.com

Copyedited by Jean Patterson
Designed by Zach Hooker
 iamabookdesigner.com
Typeset in Metro Nova Pro by Jennifer Sugden
Proofread by Anne Lucke
Color management by iocolor, Seattle
Printed and bound in China by C&C Offset Printing Co.

Front and back covers: A selection of handcrafted surfboards, 1945–2013. Photos by Ryan Field
Page 1: Rich Pavel hand shapes a fish design out of a polyurethane foam blank. San Diego, 2006. Photo by Scott Sullivan
Pages 2–3: Raymond Hookano Jr. with his *paipo* board. Ehukai beach, Oahu, 2006. Photo by Greg Betz
Pages 4–5: Richard Kenvin riding a fish surfboard shaped by Rich Pavel. Baja California Sur, 2005. Photo by Scott Sullivan

CONTENTS

FOREWORD

The legendary San Diego surfboard shaper Carl Ekstrom showed his prototype orange-fiberglass chair based on two boogie boards in the Museum's exhibition of 2011–12 entitled San Diego's Craft Revolution—From Post-War Modern to California Design. That chair has since entered Mingei International's collection as a gift of the artist. Ekstrom's other significant gift to the Museum at that time was introducing Richard Kenvin to us all. A lifelong surfer, surfboard shaper, and surf writer, Kenvin has taken us on a journey of discovery and insight that has been enriching for all involved. There is joy and satisfaction in presenting to the public the results of Kenvin's lifelong passion and work of many years in the form of the exhibition and publication *Surf Craft*.

Sōetsu Yanagi, almost a century ago, first urged people, "Ima, miyo!" ("Just now, look!"), in order to discover with fresh eyes the great beauty—the art—in the most common, ordinary, simple objects of their lives—what he called *mingei*, everybody's art. In his essays, which were translated into English in the collection called *The Unknown Craftsman*, Yanagi's ideas continue to resensitize people to the profound beauty of a simple hand broom made from natural fiber, of an old, slumped clay bowl, and of a hand-woven, indigo-dyed cotton work coat.

"The last thing a fish would notice would be water," says the Zen-like adage. It's a reminder that many of us tend to be unaware of our day-to-day context, that we easily become desensitized to the environment, the objects, and, yes, even the people who are part of our regular lives.

The first thing visitors to Southern California might notice is its ubiquitous surfboard and surf culture. With this publication and exhibition, however, Kenvin invites us to look with fresh eyes at the boards, at the early history of their design documented here after being nearly lost, and at how old principles are able, at last, to influence contemporary board design. An admirer of Yanagi's thinking about beauty, Kenvin connects *mingei* principles and traditional board shaping so deftly and appropriately that we all can gain new awareness of the art of the board, the creativity and skill of the shaper, and the joy of the ride that so connects rider and board with each other, with the surf, and with life itself that—as with the experience of great art and the other high points of life—we call it bliss.

ROB SIDNER
Director, Mingei International Museum

AUTHOR'S ACKNOWLEDGMENTS

This book evolved in conjunction with the Surf Craft exhibition held at Mingei International Museum in 2014. Over the past decade, I have been exploring surfing and surfboards in the context of traditional Hawaiian boards, Bob Simmons and his planing hulls, and Steve Lis and his fish. I have traveled all over California, Hawai'i, and Australia seeking out those who had the knowledge. I've seen the eyes of men in their eighties light up with a mischievous twinkle as they impersonated Simmons's cackling laughter, only to darken and well up with tears in mournful memory of their long-departed friend. I am deeply grateful for their time and for sharing what I consider to be sacred and often deeply personal memories and perspectives with me. The following individuals have shared their experiences with me, and their lives have shaped the content of this book: Ruth Hilts (sister of Bob Simmons), Rick Hilts (nephew of Bob Simmons), Mark Richards (interview conducted by Andrew Kidman, 2005), Reno Abellira, Peter Townend, Steve and Betsy Lis, John Elwell, Carl and Denise Ekstrom, Martha Longenecker, Al Nelson, Woody Ekstrom, Mikko Fleming, Roger Raffee, Pat Curren, Joe Curren, Skip Frye, Bud E. Rowe, Jeff Ching, Wally Froiseth, Joe and Jo Roper, Kit Horn and sons, Peter Cole, William "Stretch" Riedel, Ray Hookano Jr., Tom Henry, Rich Pavel, Steve and Cher Pendarvis, Larry Mabile, Ben Aipa, Tony Alva, Valentine Ching (interview conducted by Cher Pendarvis), Larry Bertlemann (interview conducted by Cher Pendarvis), Michael Early, Frank Nasworthy, Stanley Pleskunas, Tom "Pohaku" Stone, "Rabbit" Kekai, Bob McTavish, Mickey Munoz, Glenn Henning, Sage Joske, Cameron Beihl, Bev Morgan, Larry Gephart, Hans Newman, David Nuuhiwa, Dick Van Straalen, Dick Linville, Esteban and Karen Bojorquez, Tom Morey, Mike Griffin, Rusty Preisendorfer, Henry Hester, George Greenough, Paul Strauch, Garth Murphy, Greg and Jed Noll, Wolfgang Nyvelt, Cyrus Sutton, Jack McCoy, Hank Warner, Ryan Burch, Lucas and Geraldine Dirkse, Tyler Warren, Jon Wegener, Michael Machemer, Chris Gentile, Kirk Gee, John Van Hamersveld, Jill Jordan, Michele Lockwood, Joe Falcone, Blain Vandenberg, Franco Rinaldi, Larry Lumbeck, Peter Halasz, Jesse Faen, Christian Beamish, Andrew Kidman, Terry Martin, John Cherry, Rex and Eric Huffman, Nick, Barry, and Eli Mirandon, Mick Mackie, Mike Casey, Joel Tudor, Nobby, Scott Stecker, Mike Sheffer, Joe Bauguess, Peter Pope, Pat Rawson, Mike Eaton, Didi Kealoha, Chris Prowse, Louise Wolf, Alex Villalobos, Anna Trent Moore, and Mark, Janet, and Daniel Thomson.

I owe special thanks to John Elwell, Carl Ekstrom, Ryan Field, Jonny Mack, Michelle Bossuot, Sean Shafer, and Ryan Thomas for their extraordinary efforts on behalf of this project.

I am deeply grateful to photographer Ryan Field for his unwavering dedication to this project over the years, for his reverence and respect for the boards and the people who made them, and for his dedication to making the finest photographs possible, no matter what the circumstances. I also owe a special thanks to Ryan's wife, Amy, for her patience and support. The same goes for Scott Sullivan and his wife, Natalie, and Andrew Kidman and his partner, Michele Lockwood.

8| I am also grateful to the following photographers for their contributions: Patrick Trefz, Joe Curren, Marshall Myrman, Aaron Goulding, Doug Wylie, Anthony Ghiglia, Soren Heil, Hilton Dawe, Michael Sangiolo, Char, John Slavin, Scott Soens, Torrey Jay, Greg Betz, Dave Frankel, Alastair McKevitt, Ben Segfried, and Ian O'Roarty.

I am grateful to Cher Pendarvis for her efforts in facilitating interviews with the following people in 2006: Kit Horn, Woody Ekstrom, Bev Morgan, Larry Bertlemann, Valentine Ching, Al Nelson, Mike Sheffer, Dick Lindville, "Rabbit" Kekai, and Jeff Ching.

I am grateful to the following institutions and individuals for allowing access to their surfboard collections: Barry Haun, Paul Strauch, Spencer Croul, Dick Metz, and the staff of the Surfing Heritage & Culture Center; Hischier family of Wavelengths surf shop; the Bernice Pauahi Bishop Museum; Eric "Bird" Huffman of Bird's Surf Shed; Larry Gephart; Fernando Aguerre; Larry Fuller; Hans Newman; Ty Ponder; Nobuhito "Nobby" Ohkawa and Nobbywood surfboards, Japan; John Isaac; and Sally Parkin and The Original Surfboard Company, England.

In the context of this project, the following surfers explored the designs of Simmons, Lis, and old Hawai'i with open-minded stoke and incredible talent: Tom Henry, Dave Rastovich, Lucas Dirkse, Ryan Burch, Daniel Thomson, Dan Malloy, Christian Beamish, Joe Curren, Max Diaz, Marco Wolfinger, Tony Alva, Joe Skoby, Chris Del Moro, Tyler Warren, Stuart Kennedy, Jen Smith, and Andrew Kidman.

I am grateful to the glassers and sanders who worked on all the boards.

I owe a special thanks to Mark Weiner for his crucial assistance with Remember the Future, an exhibit of surfboards displayed in 2011 as part of Pacific Standard Time: Art in L.A. 1945–1980. This exhibit was instrumental in leading to the exhibit at Mingei International Museum.

I owe a special thanks to Christine Knoke and Rob Sidner from Mingei International Museum for seeing surfboards in the context of *mingei* and for tirelessly and patiently facilitating both the book and the exhibit of Surf Craft. I am grateful to my editor, Jean Patterson, for her patience and efforts on behalf of this book. I wish to thank the late Martha Longenecker, founder of Mingei International Museum, for sharing her insights and perspectives on Sōetsu Yanagi and the *mingei* philosophy with me. I am grateful to Brian Boennighausen, "Cho" Nagakura, Moto, and Mino and Makoto Sato for facilitating two wonderful trips to Japan and for taking me to the Nihon Mingeikan in Tokyo in 2009.

I am grateful to the following people for their friendship and support: Jonny Mack, Scott Sullivan, Mark Weiner, Ame Curtiss, Liza Richardson, Ryan Thomas, Dessa Kirk, Mary Soriano, John Singleton, Peter Clark, Sara Elwell, Greg Shobe, Cricket Wheeler, Tim O'Rourke, Chris Ahrens, Dave Frankel, Geraldine Dirkse, Joe Skoby, Andrew Kidman, Scott Hulet, and David and Dawn Inglish.

Lastly, I would like to thank Michelle Bossuot for her love, patience, and support, and my family for the same.

BIBLIOGRAPHY

Brown, DeSoto. *Surfing: Historic Photographs from Bishop Museum Archives*. Honolulu, Hawai'i: Bishop Museum Press, 2006.

Clark, John R. K. *Hawaiian Surfing: Traditions from the Past*. Honolulu: University of Hawai'i Press, 2011.

Cook, James. *The Explorations of Captain James Cook in the Pacific, as Told by Selections of His Own Journals, 1768–1779*, edited by A. Grenfell Price. New York: Heritage Press, 1958.

———. *The Voyages of Captain Cook*, edited by Ernest Rhys. Ware: Wordsworth Classics, 1999.

DeLaVega, Timothy Tovar. *Surfing in Hawai'i, 1778–1930*. Charleston, S.C.: Arcadia Publishing, 2011.

Finney, Ben R., and James D. Houston. *Surfing: A History of the Ancient Hawaiian Sport*. San Francisco: Pomegranate Artbooks, 1996. Revised edition of *Surfing, the Sport of Hawaiian Kings*. Rutland, Vt.: C. E. Tuttle Co., 1966.

Gault-Williams, Malcolm. *Legendary Surfers: A Definitive History of Surfing's Culture*. http://www.legendarysurfers.com.

Hawaiian Boarding Company website. http://www.hawaiibc.com.

Hydrodynamica website. http://www.hydrodynamica.com.

Kampion, Drew. *Stoked: A History of Surf Culture*. Santa Monica, Calif.: General Pub. Group, 1997.

Lord, Lindsay. *Naval Architecture of Planing Hulls*. New York: Cornell Maritime Press, 1946.

Mingei International Museum website. http://www.mingei.org.

Mullins, Joseph G. *Hawaiian Journey*. Honolulu, Hawai'i: Mutual Publishing, 1978.

My Paipo Boards and . . . More website. http://www.mypaipoboards.org.

Nerdrum, Odd. *On Kitsch*. Oslo: Kagge, 2000.

Patterson, Otto B. *Surf-Riding, Its Thrills and Techniques*. Rutland, Vt.: Charles E. Tuttle, 1960.

Phillips, Lisa. *The American Century: Art & Culture, 1950–2000*. New York: Whitney Museum of American Art in association with W. W. Norton, 1999.

Pods for Primates: A Catalogue of Surfboards in Australia. http://www.surfresearch.com.au.

Salmond, Anne. *The Trial of the Cannibal Dog: The Remarkable Story of Captain Cook's Encounters in the South Seas*. New Haven, Conn.: Yale University Press, 2003.

The Surfer's Journal. http://www.surfersjournal.com.

Surfing Heritage & Culture Center website. http://www.surfingheritage.org.

Surfline website. http://www.surfline.com.

Verge, Arthur C. "George Freeth: King of the Surfers and California's Forgotten Hero." *California History* 80, nos. 2 and 3 (2001): 82–105.

Warshaw, Matt. *Encyclopedia of Surfing*. http://www.encyclopediaofsurfing.com.

Yanagi, Soetsu. *The Unknown Craftsman: A Japanese Insight into Beauty*. Tokyo: Kodansha International, 1972.

Surfboards and Mingei The Unknown Craftsman

In September 2012, the directors of San Diego's Mingei International Museum invited me to curate an exhibition of surfboards at the Museum's facility in Balboa Park. The boards, which would be displayed through January 2015 in conjunction with the Balboa Park Centennial Celebration, were to occupy the Museum's entire first-floor gallery. I accepted the offer with gratitude, enthusiasm, and a sobering sense of responsibility. Here was a chance to present surfboards in their historical context of craft and design, guided by the philosophies and ideals expressed by the founder of the *mingei* movement, Sōetsu Yanagi, in his seminal work, *The Unknown Craftsman*.

Curating surfboards according to the aesthetic standards of an early twentieth-century Japanese intellectual may seem like an overly highbrow treatment of lowbrow subject matter. This is understandable. When the surfboard became a mass-produced item in the early 1960s, a centuries-old ritual craft loaded with spiritual significance migrated into the territory of commercialism. In the realm of popular culture, surfboards became disposable products of a casual pastime, soon becoming outmoded. Once made of

The simple joy of wave riding in Papua New Guinea, 2010. Photo by Char

wood, they were now composed of fiberglass and a stew of petrochemicals. Today, with the rise of professional surfing and the multibillion-dollar surf industry that supports it, surfboards have become moving billboards for action sportsters to showcase their athletic skills for the benefit of their sponsors and their careers. At best, in the commercial arena, surfboards are taken seriously as a genre of collectable memorabilia. All of these "lowbrow" perceptions of surfboards reflect the realities of surfing, but only in the context of the surfboard as an item manufactured by an industry serving a market.

Many surfers embrace these commercial realities and thrive within them. Some, including professionals and those who work in the surf industry, accept them as a necessary evil, even as they hold values that run contrary to mainstream consumerism. Still others see symptoms of a disease they would rather not be infected with, and they choose to identify with the full scope of surfing beyond its commercial distortions. They create surfboards that reflect aesthetics predating the commercial era. And more and more, there are those surfers—most notably native Hawaiians, but

Researching the roots of *mingei*. Richard Kenvin with an *alaia*-inspired paulownia wood board in front of the Japan Folk Crafts Museum (Nihon Mingeikan) in Tokyo, 2009. Photo by Char

(Opposite) A timeless scene unfolds in Papua New Guinea, where two boys slide waves on simple wooden boards, 2010. Photos by Char

also enthusiasts from other lands where surfing has spread—who are digging deep into their surfing heritage in order to balance a lopsided equation. Most surfers, though, are too busy working, living life, and surfing to split aesthetic and cultural hairs on dry land. They just want a good board.

The surfboard is a prime example of a handcrafted object that has faced challenges in maintaining its cultural role during the industrial era. In *The Unknown Craftsman*, the Japanese philosopher Sōetsu Yanagi assigns a lofty "standard of beauty" to such traditional objects but also accepts that industrialization has become the primary means of providing society with affordable goods for daily living. His ruminations in *The Unknown Craftsman* outline an aesthetic standard that is intellectually complex, yet also spiritual and, above all, practical. Handcrafts are revered as a sacred facet of human life, but they also serve as the starting point for good design, the best defense against the potentially dehumanizing effects of mass production. Yanagi does not naively propose that modern society return to a feudal system, with useful products made by a legion of nameless craftspeople toiling in obscurity. Rather, he envisions a future in which handcraftsmanship and technology are in symbiotic harmony.

Yanagi looks first to the past, and next to the present, to achieve this. In *The Unknown Craftsman*, he repeatedly stresses the importance of contemporary artist-craftsmen humbly and respectfully contemplating the unsigned, egoless work of past masters. For him, objects like the Kizaemon Ido tea bowl from sixteenth-century Korea carry the eternal message of handcrafted beauty and functional design. As the potter Bernard Leach states in the introduction to *The Unknown Craftsman*, "We can relate the work of individuals to the magnificent communal creations of unknown, humble . . . artisans of past ages and draw inspiration from them."

Jumping to the present, Yanagi extols the Danish industrial designers of the 1950s, along with American designers Ray and Charles Eames, and he cites them as showing the way forward through their work methods, in which handcrafted prototypes play a vital role in product design. Yanagi and two of his disciples, Leach and Shoji Hamada, visited Charles Eames in Los Angeles in 1954.

In the introduction to *The Unknown Craftsman*, Leach writes how Yanagi and Hamada were struck by Eames's "open acceptance both of the contemporary scientific and industrial world as well as the traditions of the past; . . . his refusal to be chained by fear, and his constant inventiveness and domination of the mechanical by a new freedom and joy in making."

Acting on an urgent impulse to protect and preserve traditional handcrafts, Yanagi coined the term *mingei*, which means "art of the people," in 1918. In 1936, along with Hamada and potter Kanjiro Kawai, he founded the Japan Folk Crafts Museum, or Nihon Mingeikan, which stands for "art of the people, returned to the people." He filled this Tokyo museum with the very objects that had inspired his philosophy. Foremost among these were Korean ceramics of the Yi dynasty (1392–1897), made in large quantities under tradition by anonymous craftsmen for five hundred years. Yanagi saw in these works a profound, transcendent beauty. In Japanese, the word that refers to this particular aesthetic of simple, subtle, unobtrusive beauty is *shibui* (adjective) or *shibusa* (noun).

Beginning in the sixteenth century, Japanese Tea masters selected similar simple

utensils while following the Way of Tea, which Yanagi considered to be the ultimate expression of *shibusa* beauty. As he states in *The Unknown Craftsman*, "We poor mortals can, with the help of this fundamental word, measure the qualities of beauty." In Yanagi's "kingdom of beauty," all objects take on their appropriate value—not in an artificial, material sense but in a human sense: naturally, eternally, and spiritually.

My own awareness of *mingei* as it relates to surfboards began in 2004, when I bought a copy of *The Unknown Craftsman* from Mingei International Museum's gift shop. At the time, I was three years into an ongoing quest to explore an obscure board design that I came to realize had a distant point of origin in two traditional Hawaiian boards: the *paha* (or *paipo*) and the *alaia*. After reading *The Unknown Craftsman*, I realized that Yanagi's manifesto about the value of handcrafts in the age of industrialism applied to the surfboards I was researching in California, and perhaps more specifically, to the traditional Hawaiian boards. Yanagi's philosophy provided a uniquely appropriate framework with which to appreciate and value all aspects of the craft, design, and use of surfboards.

In *The Unknown Craftsman*, Yanagi divides crafts into four broad categories: *mingei* (or folk) crafts, artist crafts, industrial crafts, and aristocratic crafts. *Mingei* crafts are anonymous, handmade objects intended for daily life. A traditional Hawaiian *paha* or *alaia* board is an example of a *mingei* craft. Artist crafts are signed, calling attention to the skills or stylized techniques of the individual who made them. In this way the maker begins to eclipse the object. A hand-shaped, custom surfboard made today by a famous "shaper" is an example of an artist craft. Industrial crafts, however, are made within the industrial system by mechanical means. The seasonal boards sold off-the-shelf at big-box stores are examples of industrial crafts. To a lesser extent, so are the branded, high-volume "production boards" made for the labels of renowned artist-craftsman shapers. Most production boards today employ a combination of techniques: the polyurethane foam blank is machine cut, then fine shaped and signed by an artist-craftsman shaper. Finally, the true "unknown craftsmen" of today, the glassers and sanders, finish it off. The glasser laminates the board with resin and

fiberglass, and the sander treats the entire board before it is glossed. The final category, aristocratic crafts, are those commissioned by the aristocracy or royalty. The traditional royal Hawaiian *olo*, made by a craftsman in service to the king, can be considered an example of an aristocratic craft.

In 2006, not long after reading *The Unknown Craftsman*, I stood in a small warehouse in Honolulu, surrounded by the Bernice Pauahi Bishop Museum's collection of traditional Hawaiian surfboards. Of the countless surfboards built and ridden by Hawaiians over the centuries, only a handful survived the cultural devastation that followed European contact. The boards that remain bear silent witness not only to systematic genocide but also to the design savvy, handcraftsmanship, and wave-riding knowledge of their makers. They are beautiful in their functional simplicity. They are anonymous, and yet they radiate a human presence. Human hands made them for a purpose, to be used. In *The Unknown Craftsman*, Yanagi writes of the essential, egoless appeal of anonymous handcrafted objects used in

West African boys with surf craft, 2008.
Photos by Joe Curren

daily life. In the realm of *mingei*, such items represent the purest expression of human creativity. Seeing the traditional boards, I felt that purity, and I could imagine nothing more beautiful than the thought of them flying across Hawaiian waves, under the feet of the people, long ago.

In Yanagi's "kingdom of beauty," objects speak for themselves, and in doing so reveal much about their makers. The priceless, anonymously made, wooden surfing artifacts at the Bishop Museum speak volumes about the original Hawaiian culture of surfing. They are the cornerstone, the point of origin for the historical record of surfing. All significant board designs of the modern era bear an ancestral link to one or more of these traditional boards. In many cases, the historic boards contain design secrets that modern surfboard designers are only now beginning to understand.

I was fascinated and humbled by an *alaia* board I saw resting on a rack at the museum. It was made of a single piece of wood that was seven to eight feet long, about the same width as a modern professional board, but with a very straight outline. The nose was gently rounded, the tail bluntly

squared. It was incredibly thin, less than an inch thick. The combination of design features, especially the extreme thinness, was completely foreign to me, and yet I knew that its hydrodynamics were profoundly functional. I could not imagine why a board with no buoyancy would be intentionally designed for surfing. It was beyond my understanding. I thought, "Whoever made this knew things I don't have a clue about." The *alaia* I was pondering had evolved over untold generations in a seafaring culture whose quantum understanding of the ocean was beyond the comprehension of the Western mind. In the words of the renowned anthropologist Wade Davis, "If you took all the genius that allowed us to put a man on the moon and applied it to an understanding of the ocean, what you would get is Polynesia."

The boards in the room could be roughly divided into two types: thicker boards with buoyancy, and thinner boards without buoyancy. Thick, buoyant boards like the *olo* were reserved for royalty. Thinner boards, like the *'ōnini* and the *alaia*, were ridden by everyone, royals and commoners alike. The *alaia* barely floated. Its design evolved not for ease of

paddling, but for maximum performance on a variety of waves. It allowed intimate access to one of the most dynamic, intense, and beautiful places on earth: the face of a Hawaiian wave. The *alaia* is the distant ancestor of today's high-performance surfboard. It was the most versatile and widely used board in traditional Hawaiian culture. Often referred to as the board of the commoners, in the context of *The Unknown Craftsman*, the *alaia* can immediately be recognized as fulfilling the highest aesthetic criteria of *mingei*: a highly functional, anonymous, handcrafted object made and used by many people in daily life.

Fishing for Answers

Bob Simmons, Malibu, late 1940s.
Photo courtesy of John Elwell

In *The Unknown Craftsman*, Yanagi addresses the urgent need to protect and preserve traditional handcrafts while ensuring their continued creation. If left unchecked, industrialization and commercialism threaten to disconnect people from their cultural heritage, with severe consequences. In surfing, such a disconnect has actually occurred. The causes for this are complex, and often tragic. The first tragedy was the decimation of the Hawaiian people through disease, religious oppression, and imperialism following European contact, and the subsequent loss of their highly evolved surfing culture. Another major tragedy—more recent, but just as relevant—was the death of Bob Simmons at age thirty-five in 1954, resulting in the premature loss of his profound mathematical insight into surfboard design. Simmons, as discussed below, is considered by many to be the father of the modern surfboard. Ironically, the disappearance of the *alaia*, and then that of Simmons's design know-how, immediately proceeds two marked rises in surfing's popularity. The *alaia* vanished in Hawai'i just as surfing was being revived there at the turn of the twentieth century. Simmons died just

before surfing truly exploded around the world in the late 1950s, when the rise of foam and fiberglass board construction coincided with the massive mainstream popularity of the Hollywood surf exploitation genre, beginning with the film *Gidget* (1959).

The *alaia* evolved over the centuries in the context of a culture that had a rich and intimate knowledge of the ocean. The Simmons "planing hull" was designed according to the collective mathematical knowledge of humankind, passed down through the millennia in written language, which allowed Simmons to build on the foundation laid by the Hawaiians. Though these two boards' evolutionary paths were very different, both shared fundamental design elements. When combined, the two design schools allowed for boards of superlative performance potential. But just as the traditional *alaia* was left in the dust of redwood planks at the turn of the twentieth century, the Simmons planing hull slid into obscurity after its maker's death in 1954.

Today, we have the advantage of being able to view surfboard evolution over the span of more than two hundred years, and it is clear that the disappearance of both the *alaia* and the Simmons planing hull left

Bob Simmons (far left), riding a dual-keel planing hull, drops in on a big day at Makaha, Hawai'i, during the winter of 1953. Photo by Scoop Tsuzuki, courtesy of John Elwell

a vacuum in surfboard design and performance. For those willing to listen, the surviving traditional Hawaiian *alaia* and the Simmons boards quietly transmit the same message. As Yanagi exhorted his pupils, "Take heed of the humble . . . there is no room for arrogance." In the simplest terms of Yanagi's philosophy, had the *alaia* and the Simmons boards continued to be made and used, a connection to a vast storehouse of board design and wave-riding knowledge would have been sustained. Reading *The Unknown Craftsman* affirmed my belief in the importance of past designs. The Yi dynasty pottery used in the Tea Ceremony was the point of origin for Yanagi's philosophy. In surfing, the point of origin is the collection of traditional boards in the Bishop Museum. The following is an attempt to chronicle how those boards helped surfing to survive, and to document how the most prolific and popular design in the seed culture of surfing, the *alaia*, eventually disappeared from use and significance.

In the years following Captain James Cook's death in Hawai'i in 1779, Kamehameha the Great conquered and united the Hawaiian Islands and formally established the Kingdom of Hawai'i in 1810. By developing alliances with the major Pacific colonial powers, Kamehameha preserved Hawai'i's independence under his rule. Over the next eighty-eight years, the House of Kamehameha and its successor, the House of Kalākaua, strove to preserve and continue native culture and ensure Hawai'i's sovereignty as an independent nation. But diseases introduced by westerners, coupled with a powerful, politically manipulative, and culturally repressive missionary presence, took a heavy toll on all facets of native life, especially among the commoners. In nineteenth-century Hawai'i, the once-prevalent *alaia* style of surfing began to decline and disappear, along with many other aspects of traditional culture.

In Hawaiian culture, surfboards were subject to *kapu*, which refers to a system of laws and regulations. The Hawaiian word *kapu* is usually translated into English as "forbidden," though it also bears the meanings of "sacred," "consecrated," and "holy." The term carries connotations of sacredness as much as forbiddance. Probably the best translation of *kapu* is "marked off," or ritually restricted. In the realm of surfing, the *kapu* system was applied to certain surfboard designs and source trees, most notably the royal *olo*. It seems that royals enjoyed restricted access to lighter, more buoyant wood, and to longer, thicker, more buoyant boards. With the collapse of the *kapu* system in the early nineteenth century, buoyant types of wood and longer boards became accessible to all. The desire to experience buoyancy and ease of paddling, once denied most surfers, may have been a major cause of the *alaia*'s decline in use. At the same time, foreign ships and whalers, hauling lumber from nonnative trees that had never been subject to such restrictions, provided a new source of building material for boards. These two factors, magnified by the general erosion of tradition, may have contributed significantly to the *alaia*'s decline in the nineteenth century and the prevalence of longer, thicker boards.

Veteran shaper Mike Casey made this *koa alaia* replica in 2006. It is shown here framed in the doorway of an old sugar mill on Oahu. Photo by Ryan Field

Surfing was practiced enthusiastically by many Hawaiian royals in the nineteenth century, from Kamehameha the Great himself, to the last king, King David Kalākaua, and his successor (following his death in 1891), Queen Lydia Liliʻuokalani. Prince Jonah Kūhiō Kalanianaʻole and Princess Victoria Kaʻiulani are two compelling examples of the continued practice of traditional surfing during the last days of the Kingdom of Hawaiʻi under the rule of the House of Kalākaua. More importantly, their political activism and heroic, passionate defense of the sovereign rights of native Hawaiians in the face of U.S. imperialism left an enduring legacy.

In 1885, Prince Jonah Kūhiō Kalanianaʻole, along with Prince David Laʻamea Kahalepouli Kawānanakoa and Prince Edward Abnel Keliʻiahonui, introduced surfing to California. The three princes surfed at the mouth of the San Lorenzo River in Santa Cruz County. Naturally, as princes, they rode royal *olo* boards, which they ordered to have cut from redwood at a local timber mill. Surfing in California was born of true Hawaiian royalty riding traditionally royal boards. Meanwhile,

in Hawaiʻi, young Princess Kaʻiulani rode a short, light, extremely thin *alaia*. Her board remains in the Bishop Museum's collection as the supreme example of the advanced hydrodynamics built into the *alaia* design.

The *alaia*, at least as a stand-up board, was being laid to rest in favor of more buoyant boards, such as the much larger and thicker *kīkoʻo* and royal *olo*. The trend away from the *alaia* adds to the significance and mystique of Princess Kaʻiulani's beautiful board. There is no photographic record of anyone actually riding such an *alaia* standing up. But there are many accounts in the oral histories of native Hawaiians and in the engravings and written accounts of Western visitors. All photos of *alaia*-style boards from the late 1800s and early 1900s show riders kneeling or prone.

Three famous photographs from the 1890s show native Hawaiians, clad in *malo* loincloths, posing with *alaia* boards. One, taken by an unknown photographer, shows a man tentatively identified as Charles Kauha, standing on the beach at Waikiki in the 1890s, with Diamond Head in the background. He holds a short, thin, beautifully proportioned *alaia* behind his back. Another group of photos taken of the same man, in roughly the

same place, are by a professional photographer named Frank Davey from around 1897. In Davey's photos, Kauha poses with a different, cruder board, though still an *alaia*. The third photograph is by a professional photographer named Theodore Severin, active in Hawaiʻi from 1886 through 1898. It shows an unidentified Hawaiian man, again clad in a *malo*, standing in front of a grass structure while holding a stunning, very thin, refined *alaia*. All of these pictures were obviously staged by the photographers, depicting intriguing specimens of the *alaia* design.

Dr. Henry C. Bolton took the earliest-known photographs of surfing on the island of Niʻihau in 1890. Bolton's photographs and written accounts provide a tantalizing glimpse into the waning days of traditional Hawaiian surfing. He reported: "The boards are eight or nine feet long, fifteen to twenty inches wide, *rather thin*, rounded at each end, and carefully smoothed." Bolton photographed the Niʻihau surfers standing in front of their boards clad in traditional *malo* loincloths. The boards appear to be of the *alaia*, *puua*, and *kīkoʻo* types. They are beautifully proportioned and refined, especially when compared to those ridden at Waikiki thirty years later. In the earliest-known photograph of people surfing, Bolton captured three of the Ni'ihau surfers in motion. Two of the surfers are riding prone; one is kneeling. All three are at speed and planing on an unbroken swell. Bolton's photographs not only predate the staged photos of Davey and Severin but also provide precious evidence of thin, refined, *alaia*-style boards being ridden by native Hawaiians.

In January 1893 the Kingdom of Hawai'i was overthrown in an illegal coup d'état. The prime instigators were U.S. citizens. Briefly reconstituted as the Republic of Hawai'i, by 1898 Hawai'i had been annexed by the United States as a territory, fulfilling the desires of the nonnative perpetrators of the coup. The injustice associated with the overthrow of the Hawaiian monarchy cannot be overstated. Princess Ka'iulani, heiress to the throne of the deposed Queen Lili'uokalani, fought valiantly in Europe and Washington, D.C., to restore native rule and sovereignty and to prevent annexation, but to no avail. On March 6, 1899, only seven months after the annexation, she died from severe rheumatism. She was twenty-three years old. Prince Jonah Kūhiō, who had ridden an *olo* off the coast of Santa Cruz a decade earlier, was imprisoned in 1895 for participating in a rebellion against the coup-installed Republic of Hawai'i. Such was the imperialist welcome to the man who had introduced surfing to California. Prince Kūhiō served a one-year prison term and then went on to advocate for native interests within the postannexation political system; he became the first and only U.S. congressional delegate of royal Hawaiian ancestry.

Annexation marked the end of native rule by the great line of chiefdoms and kingdoms going back to the arrival of the first navigators from the south at least a thousand years ago. In this tragic context, Princess Ka'iulani and her *alaia* become haunting metaphors for the decimation, and yet survival, of native Hawaiian culture. Just a few years after her death, surfing would experience its first boom in popularity—not only on Hawaiian shores but also in such far-flung places as California and Australia. In a bitter, ironic twist, surfing would be marketed as the Hawaiian "sport of kings," even as the Kingdom of Hawai'i ceased to exist and its monarchs and people had become disenfranchised. The prolific "national pastime" of all Hawaiians, who employed a plethora of surfboard designs (as described in ancient native stories and con-firmed by early Western visitors), had vanished. Board design would be dominated by the *olo* and the *kīko'o*: long, buoyant boards that reflected only one facet of a formerly diverse and dynamic athletic endeavor.

Into this milieu stepped the two most prominent surfers of the revival period, George Freeth and Duke Kahanamoku. Both were heroic figures whose lives transcended the injustice of their time. They were born on O'ahu in the late nineteenth century, during the final years of the Kingdom of Hawai'i, but they would come of age and share Hawaiian surfing with the world as citizens of a territorial possession of the United States. During their youth, Hawai'i went from being a sovereign kingdom to a puppet republic to an annexed territorial possession. Neither one was far removed from Hawaiian royalty. Freeth's mother was half-Hawaiian; her mother was pure Hawaiian and had given birth to three daughters fathered by Scottish businessman Archibald Cleghorn, who later fathered Princess Ka'iulani with his wife, Princess Miriam Likelike. Duke was of pure Hawaiian descent, from a family line of lower nobility who were traditionally in service to royalty.

Duke was named after his father, Duke Halapu Kahanamoku, who was christened by Princess Bernice Pauahi Bishop in honor of Prince Alfred, Duke of Edinburgh, who was visiting Hawaiʻi at the time. The princess was a direct descendant of Kamehameha I, though she refused the crown offered her by Kamehameha V upon his deathbed; this allowed the house of Kalākaua to rise to power in the final days of the monarchy. She died on October 16, 1884 (Princess Kaʻiulani's ninth birthday). The Bishop Museum is part of her legacy, founded in 1889 by her husband, Charles Reed Bishop. The impressive *olo* surfboards of her father, Chief Abner Pākī, are among the oldest surfboards in the Museum's collection, dating from 1830 and earlier.

Surfing's revival revolved around two Waikiki clubs: Alexander Hume Ford's predominantly haole (white) Outrigger Canoe Club and the Hui Nalu, or Club of the Waves, founded by native Hawaiians. Freeth, who was accepted by Ford and his cohorts, was one of the premier surfers representing the Outrigger Club. Duke was one of the founders of the Hui Nalu. The two clubs competed against each other, and Duke and Freeth were good friends, despite the apparently discriminatory atmosphere surrounding the early days of the Outrigger Canoe Club.

In 1907 Ford introduced Freeth to the famous novelist Jack London. Seeing Freeth and other Waikiki surfers in action inspired London to try surfing himself and to pen a piece about this obscure (and to London, highly exotic and appealing) lifestyle. The piece was published in the *Woman's Home Companion*. To London, Freeth was a "bronzed Mercury" partaking in "a royal sport for the natural kings of the earth." London's article caught the attention of California railroad magnate and real estate mogul Henry E. Huntington, who promptly booked Freeth passage to Los Angeles and hired him to promote his new Los Angeles–Redondo Beach rail line. The twenty-four-year-old Freeth gave surfing demonstrations at the line's terminus in Redondo Beach, causing a sensation. The "sport of kings" had officially arrived in Southern California, with prophetically commercial undertones. Barely twelve years had passed since Prince Jonah Kūhiō, one of three Hawaiian royals to first surf in California at Santa Cruz, had been thrown in a Hawaiian prison for attempting to defend his kingdom.

The boards Freeth rode, and many of the other boards used at the Outrigger Canoe Club, were vague echoes of the *kīkoʻo*. They also bore similarities to the *alaia*, but with too much thickness and width, missing the key design features of flexible thinness in combination with just the right amount of width, parallel rails, and breakaway edges. A breakaway edge is a "hard" edge, as opposed to a rounded one, located toward the tail of the board, on the bottom. The nose was also exaggerated in width. Eventually, these boards came to be known as "planks." There are examples of thin boards from the time, but they are far too wide to function like the traditional *alaia*.

Meanwhile, Duke, who was seven years younger than Freeth, was coming into his own as a surfer and swimmer, all the while representing the Hui Nalu. In 1912, at age twenty-two, he qualified for the U.S. Olympic swimming team. At the Summer Olympics that year in Stockholm, Sweden, Duke won the gold medal in the 100-meter freestyle and took silver with the relay team. On this grand stage, Duke was catapulted into international stardom. His surfing prowess and Hawaiian ancestry only served to deepen his allure and mystique, and the world loved him. In the regal personages of Duke Kahanamoku and George Freeth, surfing was burned into the consciousness of Western society as never before.

Duke went to California that year, giving surfing and swimming demonstrations and reinforcing the dazzling attraction of surfing evidenced by Freeth before him. In 1913 he traveled to the Southern Hemisphere and shared surfing with Australia, crafting a board from pine. He missed the opportunity to compete in the 1916 Summer Olympics in Berlin because they were cancelled, owing to the outbreak of World War I. During the war, he swam in exhibition races in thirty cities throughout the United States and Canada to boost morale and raise money for Liberty Bonds.

Freeth, meanwhile, continued surfing in Hawai'i and California. He became the first official lifeguard in the United States, performing many heroic rescues, deeds that did not go unnoticed in the wake of the sinking of the *Titanic* in 1912. But in 1919, Freeth became a victim of the Spanish influenza pandemic, fell ill, and died on April 7 in a nursing facility, the Agnew Sanitarium in downtown San Diego. He was thirty-four years old.

In 1920, at the dawn of the most glamorous and hedonistic decade of the twentieth century, Duke won gold medals in both the 100-meter freestyle and the relay at the Summer Olympics in Antwerp, Belgium. On the way back from this glorious performance, Duke passed through Detroit, where a young swimmer named Tom Blake intercepted him and shook his hand at a theater screening of Duke's Olympic swim races. Blake, who greatly admired Duke, later headed to Waikiki to fulfill his dream of surfing in Hawai'i alongside his hero. Blake, a transplanted haole kid from the Midwest, walked in Duke's footsteps as closely as anyone.

Just over twenty years had passed since the death of Princess Ka'iulani. Her *alaia*, stored safely somewhere on O'ahu, quietly kept its secrets where it lay. Ironically, the *olo*-riding, formerly imprisoned Prince Jonah Kūhiō, still a congressional delegate for the Territory of Hawai'i, put the first bill for Hawaiian statehood before the U.S. Congress in 1919. The prince died in 1922, addressing issues of native land use right up until the end.

Duke and Blake defined surfing in the 1920s and early 1930s, and for them, the foundational surfboard design was the *olo*. Duke had ridden an *olo*-style board in his youth that was sixteen feet long, made of *koa*, and weighed 114 pounds. Buoyancy and momentum were the driving forces behind such a board. Duke possessed all the positive characteristics of a noble aristocrat: he was heroic, athletic, cultured, well-traveled, humble, relaxed, and gentlemanly. He was the perfect ambassador for Hawai'i, and for surfing. He was often assumed to be of royal Hawaiian ancestry, which intensified the connotations associated with surfing's revival in the public eye. There was nothing more kingly, in the best sense of the word, than "the Duke" gliding on a sixteen-foot *olo*, pursuing his birthright, the "sport of kings." In the aftermath of World War I, in which mechanized warfare, brutal "human wave attacks," and industrial-scale death had marked the ultimate outcome of an endless power struggle defined by nobility, Duke was a gentle salve to a weary public. The military-industrial complex had reduced young men to mere particles in waves of slaughter on the battlefields of Europe. Duke was a vision of sanity, mastering a natural wave in an affirmation of life, instead of becoming part of an unnatural one in a trail of death.

Later, Duke rode *kīko'o*-style boards, shorter and wider than the *olo*, but still substantial. Today these boards, like Freeth's, are often referred to as "planks." They are very heavy and, like the *olo*, operate off buoyancy and momentum, with the added factor of an ample planing surface through a wide tail. Often made of redwood and pine, these planks became widely used as surfing spread throughout California and Australia.

When Blake visited the Bishop Museum on his first trip to Hawai'i in 1924, the traditional surfboards he saw there made a deep and lasting impression on him. He returned to Hawai'i in 1926, where paddle racing was a competitive staple between the Outrigger Canoe Club and the Hui Nalu. Blake excelled as a paddler, and as such, was immediately intrigued by the paddling potential of the two massive *olo* boards of Chief Abner Pākī he had seen at the Bishop Museum. At the time, Chief Pākī's boards were in disrepair and in need of restoration. Blake offered to restore them for the museum. After some initial resistance, the museum authorities granted him permission. In the process, he developed a serious *olo* fetish. Blake said of this experience, "I . . . wondered about these boards in the Museum, wondered so much that in 1926 I built a duplicate of them as an experiment, my object being not to make a better board, but to find a faster board to use in the annual and popular surfboard paddling races held in Southern California each summer." Blake went on to handcraft a magnificent sixteen-foot solid redwood reproduction of an *olo*; he proceeded to use it to win the paddle races. He then designed a hollow, box-railed version, which he called the "Hawaiian Hollow Surfboard." He patented his invention in 1930 and sold it commercially as a kit. Advertisements touted its "streamlined" design and its "air chamber." More paddleboard than surfboard, Blake's pintailed shape would nevertheless have an influence on surfboard design, especially the narrow tail. In 1935, Blake designed and patented a small "keel" fin to give his boards more directional stability.

Blake is rightfully recognized as a legendary figure in surfing's revival. His deep reverence for traditional Hawaiian boards and culture, his handcraftsmanship, his ingenuity, and his love for surfing reflected his own mystical quest for an ever-deeper connection

Wally Froiseth at home in Honolulu, sharing his experiences with hot curl and *paipo* boards, October 2006. Photo by Greg Betz

to nature. He was an extraordinarily romantic figure, gliding gracefully across the waves of Waikiki on hand-hewn wooden planks, *olo* boards, and hollow paddleboards. But from a design perspective, his hollow, square-railed, narrow-tailed "surfboards" were better suited for winning paddle races than for riding waves. Blake's obsession with the *olo* inadvertently continued to sever surfing's connection to the *alaia*—the effect being that the *alaia*, the most widely used and popular board in traditional Hawaiian culture, remained irrelevant. In the original culture, the *olo* was a highly specialized board used by the elite for a specific type of surf, while the *alaia* was a versatile design used by everyone.

The year 1919 was an auspicious one for surfing, apart from the tragic death of George Freeth. That year, John Kelly, Wally Froiseth, and Bob Simmons were born in California. Largely through these individuals and their friends, surfing would move out of the plank-and-paddleboard era of the "royal" revival period and begin its long and roundabout journey toward rediscovering the lost hydrodynamic secrets of the "commoner"

boards. Blake's use of fins, his streamlined paddleboard shapes, and the collection of traditional boards he helped restore for the Bishop Museum would all come into play for very different reasons. But by 1950, only the fin and the pintail would remain in use as legacies of Blake. Everything else had been transformed.

The first major step occurred in 1934, when Fran Heath, John Kelly, and Wally Froiseth came up with an entirely new design called the "hot curl," in Hawai'i. Neither *olo* nor *alaia* nor plank nor paddleboard, the hot curl nevertheless had a little in common with all of them. Though Heath, Kelly, and Froiseth were protégés of Blake in many ways, they found that planks and box-railed hollow paddleboards did not work well in the larger, more challenging surf they were riding at breaks beyond Waikiki. Like Blake, whom they surfed with and admired, they spent time examining the traditional *olo* and *alaia* boards in the Bishop Museum. In the hot curl shape are distant echoes of the *olo*,

along with a remarkable resemblance to the lesser-known *kīoe* design.

The hot curl was literally born from the plank. Initially, the hot curlers cut down and modified existing planks by narrowing and "pulling in" the nose and tail, cutting a "V" into the bottom of the tail, which blended into a forgiving rolled bottom with soft, upturned rails. The narrow, streamlined template, coupled with the pulled "V" tail, created suction that held the board in trim in the critical pocket of the wave face. Blake's streamlined pintail found its way into the hot curl, but his square box rails did not. Whereas square-railed planks and paddleboards would drift sideways toward inevitable disaster, the hot curl held and maintained control. A skilled rider like "Rabbit" Kekai, for example, could engage a finless hot curl in fast lateral trim, and then break trim with a controlled slide, before setting the rail back into trim and speeding down the line. This kind of surfing

Simmons's 1936 Ford, parked at Marine Street in La Jolla, 1954. The car served as both transportation and living quarters as he scoured the California coast for surf. The beautiful running lines of his planing hull surfboard, resting on the roof, are clearly visible. Photo by John Elwell

Bob Simmons talks design with other surfers at Marine Street in La Jolla, January 1954. Photo by John Elwell

had not been seen in the islands since the days of the *alaia*. Heralded as a revolutionary style of "hot-dog" surfing, it can also be understood, perhaps more relevantly, as a return to the traditional style that was snuffed out in the nineteenth century. Hawaiian in origin, the hot curl marked a turn away from the revival era toward the lost styles, techniques, and designs of surfing's past.

In 1939, the story of Bob Simmons, at least in the realm of surfing, begins. Simmons, too, would tap into design principles found in the traditional boards, but it would be mathematics, not proximity to the Bishop Museum's collection, that led him there. His calculations led not to the *olo*, but to the *paha* and the *alaia*, the boards of the commoners. As a young man, Simmons was severely injured in a bicycle accident and nearly lost his left arm. While in the hospital, a fellow patient who happened to be a surfer recommended that he try paddling a surfboard as therapy to regain the use of his arm. Fascinated by the surfer's tales, and highly motivated to save

his arm, Simmons purchased a surfboard kit when he was released from the hospital. The kit Simmons bought was for a Tom Blake Hawaiian Hollow Surfboard, which, with help from his sister Ruth, he assembled in the garage of his family's home in Los Angeles.

Simmons took to paddling the board off Balboa Island in Newport Bay, gradually gaining strength and partial usage of his arm. Eventually, he took the board in the ocean and tried to surf. The experience left Simmons unconvinced that a design such as Blake's was the best solution for surfing. In fact, for the rest of his life, he used the word "paddleboard" as a derogatory term, usually applying it to what he considered nonfunctional surfboard design. After studying engineering at the California Institute of Technology and working for Douglas Aircraft during World War II, Simmons set about applying his truly rare, mathematically inclined intellect to the task of making boards that were better suited for surfing.

Like the hot curlers, Simmons began by modifying existing redwood planks. He kept the wide tails and changed everything else.

Unlike the hot curlers, Simmons saw narrow, pulled-in tails as a problem. Simmons had never seen a hot curl, but he saw plenty of paddleboards in California. He considered them hydrodynamic "disasters." Simmons arrived at an outline shape with a rounded nose and nearly parallel running lines, ending in a wide, squared-off tail. This was remarkably similar in outline to the *alaia* of old. Once the template was established, Simmons added camber—a slightly upturned convexity called a "spoon"—to the noses, solving a number of problems. Now Simmons dealt with the rails. By applying wing theory, he designed rails that generated dynamic lift, just as in aeronautics. Unlike the finless hot curl—which held in by suction and calculated drag—or the finless *alaia*—which held in by flex and friction—the Simmons rail held in by using fins. In this way, he harnessed not only the *alaia*-like planing surface of his boards, but also the lift-generating rails.

Simmons's design was, in the simplest terms, an application of Western science to the latent powers in Princess Ka'iulani's *alaia*. The design principles of the *alaia* found their way into Simmons's boards through an

Lindsay Lord's study on planing hulls, *Naval Architecture of Planing Hulls*, Cornell Maritime Press, 1946. This book was a crucial source of information for Bob Simmons.

Illustrations showing Lord's planing plates in motion on the surface of Pearl Harbor, Oahu. Note the universal *paipo*/bodyboard shape of aspect ratio A6, the definitive speed generator for surfboard design.

unlikely source: a study on powered planing hull boats commissioned by the U.S. Navy in 1945. Lindsay Lord, a naval architect known for designing ultrafast rumrunners during Prohibition, was hired by the Navy to conduct the study. Prior to Lord's work, nearly all scientific data on hull performance in seagoing vessels was associated with displacement hull designs. The scientific study of planing hulls was an entirely new field of research. Fittingly, the venue for the tests was Pearl Harbor, on O'ahu. Lord's findings were published in 1946 in a textbook titled *Naval Architecture of Planing Hulls*.

In the study, Lord gathered data from a series of model "plates" that he towed across the surface of Pearl Harbor. The plates were designed and built by Lord with assistance from H. A. Loveland and Wilson Lee of the Pearl Harbor Boat Shop. Tested for their planing performance, the models used in the study were similar in design to traditional Hawaiian surfboards. The fastest designs had an aspect ratio (that is, the proportion between their width and length) that mirrored that of the traditional *alaia* and *paha*. The *alaia* can be found in plate A3 (Aspect ratio 3),

which Lord considered to have superb potential for seagoing planing hulls. The *paipo*, a twentieth-century incarnation of the traditional *paha* design, makes a conspicuous appearance in plate A6 (Aspect ratio 6), which Lord found to be the fastest of them all.

Simmons used Lord's data to build the same highly effective speed-generating aspect ratios into his planing hull surfboard designs. To harness and control the speed, he looked to airfoil data such as that published in 1949 in Ira H. Abbott's *Theory of Wing Sections*. Armed with the latest scientific studies on planing hulls and wing design, Simmons applied mathematical formulas to develop boards that used parallel-railed templates and aspect ratios similar to the *alaia*-like planing plates in Lord's study. He added a cambered displacement hull in the forward third of the board, blending into a flat or concave planing hull in the rear two-thirds. He designed rounded, aerodynamic rails that generated lift, like a boomerang or an airplane wing. He looked to torpedo design, as well as feathered arrows, to design and position fins on his boards. These were used on each side of the board, near the tail, to harness and control the speed created

by the board's planing hull, parallel running lines, and lift-generating rails. Simmons referred to these boards as hydrodynamic planing hulls, or simply "machines." His use of multiple fins, lifting rails, and a calculated wetted planing surface was unprecedented. All of it was determined by mathematics and scientific theory.

Materials were also at issue. In the late 1940s, the use of such materials as balsa wood, Styrofoam, resin, and fiberglass was pioneered in California by Pete Peterson, Joe Quigg, and Simmons. This brought about a revolution in lightness. In 1948, hot curlers Wally Froiseth and George Downing left Hawai'i and sailed to California. While surfing at Malibu, Downing lost his board into the pier, breaking part of the nose off. Simmons was surfing Malibu that day, too, and witnessed the damage to Downing's board. He approached Downing and offered to show him a way to repair his damaged board using resin and fiberglass.

Downing's board was repaired, and the knowledge of working with these new materials was passed on. The result was that the hot curl could now be successfully finned. Downing had been working on a fin box for the hot curl, and resin and fiberglass

Boomerangs made by Bob Simmons, late 1940s. Simmons explored the relationship between the leading edge airfoil of his boomerangs and the rails of his surfboards, both of which created dynamic lift. Collection of John Elwell. Photo by Ryan Field

Simmons planing hull, Morro Bay, California, 2005. Board from the Hischier family collection (also shown on page 75). Photo by Andrew Kidman

Bob Simmons at Malibu, June 5, 1951. He is riding a dual-finned hydrodynamic planing hull. Photo courtesy of Woody Ekstrom

Windansea surfers wait for a set, 1949. The defiant double flip off reflects the renegade, individualistic mentality of surfers like Gard Chapin, Bob Simmons, and Miki Dora in the 1940s and 1950s. By the late 1970s, skateboarders and punks had become the outlaws, and surfers sought "respectability." Photo courtesy of Woody Ekstrom

From left: "Mini" Simmons planing hull by Joe Bauguess, 2006; short balsa single fin by Joe Quigg, early 1950s; red pintail by Matt Kivlin, 1952; dual-keel, concave balsa planing hull by Bob Simmons, 1950. Many design features present in modern boards can be seen in the early designs of Quigg, Kivlin, and Simmons. Collection of Fernando Aguerre. Photo by Ryan Field

provided a successful solution to attach a fin. The golden era of finless hot curl surfing, with its fleeting glimpse of the old Hawaiian style of surfing, was ending, with the introduction of the single-finned, big-wave "gun" and the single-finned Malibu "potato chip" board created by Quigg. As the finned hot curl morphed into the big-wave gun, it allowed access to bigger and hollower surf in Hawai'i, while the Malibu chip allowed for the pivot and trim "longboard" style of "hot-dogging" to develop in California. This marked the start of the single-fin era, which would last for thirty years.

Back in Hawai'i, Froiseth, Downing, and the hot curlers continued to develop their design. A great deal of cross-pollination occurred as California surfers like Quigg visited Hawai'i and added hot curl elements to their single-fin designs. Simmons spent nine months on O'ahu in 1953, surfing on occasion with Froiseth and the hot curl crew. From a design standpoint, though, he maintained his independence. His wide, dual-finned planing hull was considered suspect by the hot curlers, especially as the hot curl, now finned, was serving them very well as they pioneered

the giant surf at Makaha, on the west side of O'ahu. Quigg and the hot curlers stuck to their path; Simmons stuck to his.

There is, however, a crucial area of common ground between Simmons and Froiseth in the form of the *paipo*, a twentieth-century incarnation of the traditional *paha* design. Inspired by watching a Hawaiian kid ride a *paipo* at Kuhio Beach at Waikiki, Froiseth started making and riding *paipo* boards for small-to-medium-sized surf. Twentieth-century *paipo* boards were usually ridden prone, as a bodyboard, with a few very notable exceptions. Froiseth and, a little later, Valentine Ching Jr. mastered the extremely difficult feat of riding the *paipo* standing up. By standing on thin, short *paipo* boards, Froiseth and Ching brought another element from the lost art of traditional surfing, on small boards, into the postrevival world of Hawaiian surfing. They proved that there was far more to board design than length and buoyancy. Something akin to magic seemed to happen when a short, thin board interacted with the wave face. As a master and innovator of both the longer, buoyant, streamlined hot curl and the

much shorter, wider, but far-less-buoyant *paipo* board, Froiseth was intuitively tapping into the lost design heritage of the traditional boards. Some of Froiseth's *paipo* boards are almost identical in shape to Lindsay Lord's A6 planing plate. Like Simmons, Froiseth found that such a design functioned best with dual fins.

After Simmons returned to California from Hawai'i in January 1954, he continued refining his planing hulls, building his finest specimens in a shed near the lifeguard station in Imperial Beach, near the mouth of the Tijuana River. Tragically, Simmons died in a surfing accident at Windansea Beach in La Jolla on September 26, 1954. The hydrodynamic planing hull design, Simmons's "scientific *alaia*," died with him. Born just days before George Freeth's death in April 1919, Simmons, like Freeth, died in San Diego at age thirty-five.

With the passing of Simmons, the "longboard" era began in California, based on the relatively light Malibu chip boards from the late 1940s and 1950s. These boards were

A rare photograph of Steve Lis riding his fish at Big Rock in La Jolla in the early 1970s. Photo by Marshall Myrman

originally made of balsa wood. They were pivot and trim single-fins, usually just under ten feet long, used for small-to-medium-sized surf. The performance carrot for the longboard era was the nose ride, in which the surfer dangled five or ten toes off the front of the board while speeding along in trim. Longboards were refined slightly and then exploded into mass production in the late 1950s, when balsa was replaced by polyure-thane foam. The popularity of the 1959 Holly-wood surf exploitation film *Gidget* ensured a market for commercially produced long-boards, and the surf industry was born. With it came design conformity, huge crowds of eager novices, and all manner of trends, fads, bells, and whistles that had little to do with functional board design and everything to do with selling surfboards.

Into this post-Gidget world of pivot and trim longboards and nose-riding came a knee-boarder named George Greenough. Hyper-creative, hyper-productive, hyper-intelligent, mildly eccentric, and supremely gifted at riding waves, Greenough almost singlehand-edly invented the modern "shortboard" style

of surfing. He rode very short, thin, flexible "spoon" designs with tapered, foiled fins. Thanks to Greenough's well-documented approach to riding waves, the longboard era soon became dead in the water. His Austra-lian friends, including Bob McTavish and Ted Spencer, began building much shorter surfboards for stand-up surfing. Before long, Greenough's new style of surfing had crossed over into the stand-up realm. The Australian surfers Nat Young and Wayne Lynch are two of the greatest examples from the famed "shortboard revolution" of the late 1960s.

Meanwhile, in Hawai'i, a completely separate design was given the shortboard treatment. This was the transformation of the big-wave gun into the "mini gun" by Dick Brewer in 1967. The modern gun shape had evolved there over a thirty-year period out of the hot curl. Brewer, himself a master shaper of big-wave guns, miniaturized the gun de-sign into a short, narrow, teardrop shape with a pintail called a mini gun, or "pocket rocket." These boards gave young Hawaiian surfers like Reno Abellira, Gerry Lopez, and Barry Kanaiaupuni access to new territory on pow-erful waves. Brewer's radical little pintails

seemed to swirl out of the same collective conscience that had spawned the short Australian boards. This development soon spread to California, where fifteen-year-old Steve Lis was already building boards in his garage; having mastered bodysurfing and bellyboarding, he was now coming into his own as a kneeboarder. It was in this rev-olutionary atmosphere that the first "fish" humbly came into being.

One day in 1967, Lis and his buddy, Stanley Pleskunas, noticed that an abandoned long-board had washed into a cave at Osprey Street in the Point Loma community of San Diego. The boys returned at low tide, salvaged the board, stripped it, and cut the blank in half. Each had half a blank to shape a kneeboard from. Lis used his half of the salvage job to shape the first fish. He made sure the tail was wide enough to accommodate his swim fins as they would be positioned when he was kneeboarding. He cut the tail into two pins, with each pintail getting its own fin, one on either side. The end result was a short, wide, twin-pinned board with dual fins.

The fish was like a pocket rocket pin-tail, doubled and mirrored, shortened and squared. Poetically born from a discarded

Reflecting on a pair of Greenough spoon boards from the 1960s. Hischier family collection. Photo by Andrew Kidman

Spoon mold built by George Greenough in the 1960s. Photo by Andrew Kidman

Clockwise, from upper right: Warren Bolster's iconic portrait of Steve Lis. San Diego, 1973. Photo by Warren Bolster

Jeff Ching prepares to accelerate on a Lis fish. San Diego, early 1970s. Photo by Warren Bolster

Big Rock kneeboarders Mark Skinner and Rex Huffman roll out the welcome mat in the early 1970s. Photo by Marshall Myrman

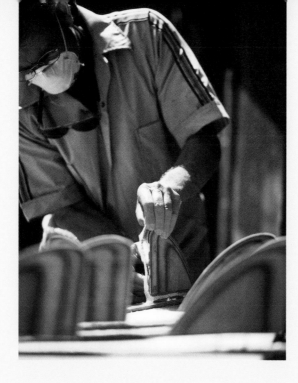

Larry Gephart, making keel fins by hand for over forty years, 2005. Photo by Andrew Kidman

longboard, it was an odd amalgamation of all the designs that had preceded it, yet greater than the sum of its parts. It operated under a different set of hydrodynamic principles than the single-fin boards did. The relationship between the ample planing surface, the rails, and the fins was far more efficient. As Lis said in 1973, "The fish does everything I could want out of foam and resin. Speed, maneuverability, and a good feel on the wave." It was a glimpse into the future of surfing, and to a certain extent, the future of skateboarding, too.

Lis's surfing on the fish was legendary and prophetic. As the venerable surf and skate photographer Warren Bolster wrote in *Surfing Magazine* in 1973: "Not since George Greenough has there been a kneeboarder who has so easily earned the respect of the surfers who have seen him. Through his development of the fish, surfers are again benefiting from the pioneering efforts of a kneeboarder. *In waves up to ten feet, Steve Lis is the best and fastest wave rider I have ever seen.*"

The first surfer to ride a Lis fish standing up was Jeff Ching, a young college student who had recently moved from Oʻahu to San Diego to attend school. Through Ching, the fish became connected to the *paipo* of Hawaiʻi. Ching grew up riding *paipo* boards, and he was mesmerized by the stand-up *paipo* riding of Valentine Ching (no relation). Seeing Lis's design, and remembering Valentine's ability to ride an even smaller board with no buoyancy, Ching became inspired to try riding Lis's kneeboard standing up. Ching experienced unprecedented speed and traction on the fish. It was a truly revolutionary moment, one of the great milestones in twentieth-century surfing, and a powerful point of contact to the traditional boards. In 1972, Jimmy Blears of Hawaiʻi rode a fish to victory in the World Championship of Surfing (an amateur event billed as "the surfing Olympics"). Such a feat would have been unthinkable just a few years before.

The fish came on the scene in 1967, the urethane skateboard wheel in 1973. In the years between these milestones, skateboards were still shackled with nonfunctional clay and steel wheels. The fish, on the other hand, gave dynamic acceleration and traction (on very small boards) to a handful of open-minded surfers. The early fish surfing of Jeff Ching, "Bunker" Spreckels, Mike Tabeling, Larry Gephart, David Nuuhiwa, and Skip Frye was a sort of aquatic foreshadowing of what the urethane wheel would later bring to skateboarding. The fish allowed them to deal with vertical and beyond-vertical terrain on the wave face in much the same way that a skilled skateboarder would ride a bowl or a pool during the early days of the urethane wheel revolution.

Surfing and skateboarding were so closely intertwined in the early years of the urethane wheel that a number of fascinating examples of connectivity, as well as personal and design relationships and influences, reveal themselves. In Hawaiʻi, Ben Aipa, working with Larry Bertlemann, "Buttons" Kaluhiokalani, and Mark Richards, "loosened" the single fin by creating the "sting" design. Aipa, inspired by watching powered planing hull boat races in Pearl Harbor, had plugged a wide planing

Left: Fish surfer Frank Nasworthy innovated the urethane skateboard wheel in the early 1970s. Here he holds a relic from the first production run. Carlsbad, California, 2008. Photo by Ryan Field

Right: Roller Derby skateboard customized to look like a Mirandon twin pin, 1968. At the time, skateboard performance lagged far behind that of surfboards like the Steve Lis fish or the twin pin. Nasworthy's wheel would bring fish-level performance to skateboarding by 1973. Collection of Hans Newman. Photo by Ryan Field

34| surface (again with an aspect ratio very similar to Lord's A6) into his boards. He did this by putting a pronounced wing up from the tail. Bertlemann and Buttons were both raised on *paipo* boards, and they translated their *paipo* riding skills into Aipa's new design. Both were also excellent skateboarders, and the urethane wheel coincided with Aipa's new sting. The result was a loose, low, and pivotal, maneuver-filled style of surfing: the surf-skate style. Eventually, the sting, along with the fish, would propel board design to culminate with Simon Anderson's "thruster," invented in 1980.

In the late 1970s, Reno Abellira brought a *paipo*-inspired, dual-finned fish-style board into the fledgling world of professional surfing. Early pro surfing was a strictly single-fin affair, with the sting emerging in the mid-1970s as the most progressive single-fin option. Like Jeff Ching, Abellira had grown up awed by Valentine Ching's stand-up *paipo* riding. Abellira was also a protégé of Froiseth. In Australia, at a large contest sponsored by Coca-Cola, Abellira rode a tiny dual-finned design into the finals. This was a crucial event in modern surfing, as it reflected the end of single-fin dominance. It also marked the reintroduction of the dual-finned concepts of Simmons, complete with their links to the lost designs of the past (as explored by Simmons and Froiseth decades earlier) into the fledgling world of pro surfing.

Abellira's performance was noticed by Mark Richards, an up-and-coming Australian pro surfer who had seen Jimmy Blears win the world championship in 1972 riding a fish. Inspired by Abellira, Richards started working with Aipa in Hawai'i, as well as Brewer, in a concentrated effort to design high-performance boards for competition. At the time of the Coca-Cola contest, Richards was riding a single-fin Aipa sting. Seeing Abellira flying across the waves on his twin-fin pushed Richards toward a twin-finned solution. By 1978, with help from Brewer, Richards had developed a twin-finned design, the "MR" twin. The MR twin had some elements of Aipa's sting, though they were moved about a bit to accommodate a dual-fin setup. In 1979 he won the world title, with the MR twin being crucial to his success. He went on to win three more world titles. As a testament to the functional power of Simmons's original concept of using outboard fins on each rail, with planing surface between them, it should be noted that after Richards, no surfer ever won the world title on a single fin again. (The last surfer to do so was Wayne Bartholomew in 1978.) By 1981, Simon Anderson had introduced the three-finned thruster design, effectively combining the best attributes of the dual-finned concepts of Simmons with the best features of the single fin. It took a long time, but the separate design schools of Simmons and the hot curlers, which had never mixed at Malibu and Makaha in the 1940s and 1950s, were finally united. Anderson's creation was an amalgamation of many designs, and it supercharged surfboard performance. It has been copied, cloned, and reproduced ad infinitum for more than thirty years, and professional surfing was, so to speak, built on its deck.

Four-time world professional surfing champion Mark Richards with two of the deadliest arrows in his late 1970s competition quiver: the Aipa sting and the MR twin, 2005. These designs helped revolutionize performance in the competitive arena of the IPS (International Professional Surfers) from 1976 through 1982. Photo by Andrew Kidman

Boards by Bob Simmons, George Greenough, Steve Lis, Stanley Pleskunas, and Skip Frye on a central California beach. Boards from the Hischier family collection. Photo by Andrew Kidman (see pages 75 and 93 for a closer look at the balsa boards shown in this photo)

Return to Genesis

The saga of surfboard design in the twentieth century, from George Freeth to Simon Anderson, was dominated by trial and error. Much of what was "pioneered" and "innovated" had already been defined, in basic principle, by the traditional Hawaiian boards and the Simmons planing hull. Over the past two decades, the connection to these "lost" designs of the past has deepened. In what Paul Strauch (a legendary Hawaiian surfer and the director of the Surfing Heritage & Culture Center) describes as a "renaissance," a new reverence for the wisdom and knowledge of the past is emerging. For today's craftspeople, this means not just studying and analyzing the old designs, but also actually building *alaia* and planing hull boards again—not to be hung on the wall as decorations, but to be put in the ocean and surfed on. Using the boards for their intended purpose, a principle critical to Yanagi's philosophy, brings them out of the realm of abstract conjecture and into the sphere of contemporary relevance.

The traditional boards preserved by the Bishop Museum have, over the past century, manifested the abstract concepts that Yanagi worked so hard to express. Without the presence of their makers, the boards themselves, simple and anonymous, have indirectly guided the evolution of surfing. This is the power of the unknown craftsman, the legacy of makers long gone and forgotten. George Freeth, Duke Kahanamoku, Tom Blake, Wally Froiseth, John Kelly, Fran Heath, and others who stood in the presence of those boards never knew their creators. But the boards spoke for themselves, and slowly but surely, those who sought them out fell under their influence.

For Froiseth, more than a century of surf history culminated in 2001 when he carefully replicated Princess Ka'iulani's *alaia*. Kelli Ann Heath, Fran Heath's granddaughter, surfed the replica at Queen's Surf in Waikiki. While this event was barely noticed amid the hustle and bustle of modern surfing at the turn of the twenty-first century, in the long view, it is a milestone of historic proportions. The perplexing, seemingly unridable *alaia*, once the most popular board in surfing, was again being ridden after more than a century. In the context of *mingei*, the work of an anonymous

Dave Rastovich rides a balsa wood replica of a circa 1950 Simmons planing hull built by John Cherry and Terry Martin, 2006. Photo by Scott Sullivan

Steve Lis makes a fish in his Ocean Beach shaping room, 2005. Photo by Scott Sullivan

past master was revered and replicated, and finally put back to use.

Two people who have played crucial roles in this surfing renaissance are Tom "Pohaku" Stone and John Elwell. Pohaku's work has focused on traditional Hawaiian boards, Elwell's on Simmons and the hydrodynamic planing hull. Since about 1994, as a direct result of their efforts, both the *alaia* design and the Simmons planing hull are once again being built and ridden around the world. For young board builders like Daniel "Tomo" Thomson and Ryan Burch, an intimate knowledge of both the *alaia* design and the Simmons planing hull has led to a new generation of ultra-high-performance surfboards. For board builders of the school of trial-and-error, like seventy-one-year-old Carl Ekstrom, new life has been breathed into old designs. A new design paradigm is emerging—one that is connected to, rather than disconnected from, the crucial, foundational design principles found in the *alaia*

and the Simmons planing hull. As Yanagi writes, handcraftsmanship and a humble reverence for the work of the unknown craftsmen of past ages show the way forward. In recent surfing history, this has certainly been the case.

Stone is always quick to point out that traditional Hawaiian surfing was not about any one specific design. It was about many designs, used on many different types of waves, employing a variety of surfing styles and techniques. Today, it is fascinating to look at the old boards in a modern context and find ancestral similarities. The ancient *uma* looks for all the world like a late-1970s skateboard deck. The early snowboards of Jake Burton and Dimitrije Milovich are nearly identical to the *alaia*. The hot curl has an ancestor in the ancient *kīoe*; Greenough's flexible fiberglass "spoon," in the thin, flexible *alaia*; Steve Lis's fish, in the *paha*.

Today, *alaia*-inspired designs have spread to every corner of the surfing world. The performance of these boards must be seen to be

believed. A modern master of the design, like Ryan Burch, performs an athletic dance that calls to mind not only surfing but also skateboarding and snowboarding. The common point of origin for all three becomes readily apparent in an ode to a truly universal design and riding style.

Surfing today is a global cultural phenomenon. Its current epoch began over two hundred years ago, when the people of the Pacific, particularly those in Hawai'i, encountered the scientific expeditions of Captain Cook. Modern surfing was born from this collision of cultures, and the effects are still being felt today—not just in the Pacific, but around the world. Cook's voyages in the Pacific marked the meeting of two vast and ancient systems of human knowledge. The Polynesians successfully related to the natural world with intelligence and intimacy. The Europeans, on the other hand, quantified and questioned nature, probing it with science and mathematics, trying to understand, and ultimately control, its forces. It was the Age of Enlightenment, and these natural forces

Japanese surfer/craftsman Yoshi rides an *alaia*-inspired finless board in Indonesia, 2010. Photo by Char

Ryan Burch rides a simple foam chunk modeled after Lindsay Lord's A5 planing plate from *Naval Architecture of Planing Hulls*. Windansea, 2009. Photo by Doug Wylie

Simmons historian John Elwell holds a dual-keel modern planing hull built by Daniel Thomson in 2010. This photo was taken in Coronado, California, not far from where Elwell first met Bob Simmons in December 1949. Photo by Doug Wylie

Opposite: Hydrodynamic planing hull replica made by Terry Martin and John Cherry, downtown San Diego, 2005. Photo by Scott Sullivan

were being defined with formulas and theories. It was also the dawn of the Industrial Revolution. Before long, the Enlightenment ideals of Cook and the Royal Society, along with the sovereignty of nearly every culture in contact with the industrialized nations of the world, would yield to the overwhelming economic and military power made possible by the Industrial Revolution.

But somehow, against all odds, surfing would not die. Today, more than ever, it remains a testament to the cultural survival of the Hawaiians, and its impact on Western European and Japanese culture is ongoing and profound. Hawai'i was, is, and will forever be the true home of surfing, with a legacy of human creativity that extends far beyond its shores. In Tahiti, not far from where Cook recorded the Transit of Venus in 1769, surfers ride a wave called Teahupo'o that is so majestic and dangerous it defies belief. In Yorkshire, England, not far from where Cook was born, rubber-clad Englishmen ride perfect waves on the shores of the North Sea. Nearby, in the Captain Cook Birthplace Museum, rests a hand-hewn traditional surfboard made by Tom "Pohaku" Stone. In what Stone calls a "change of seasons," surfing has finally come full circle. And whether they know it or not, the rubber-clad Englishmen of Yorkshire and the Jet Ski–assisted heroes tackling super waves in Tahiti ride on boards that will forever be related to the work of unknown craftsmen of distant ages.

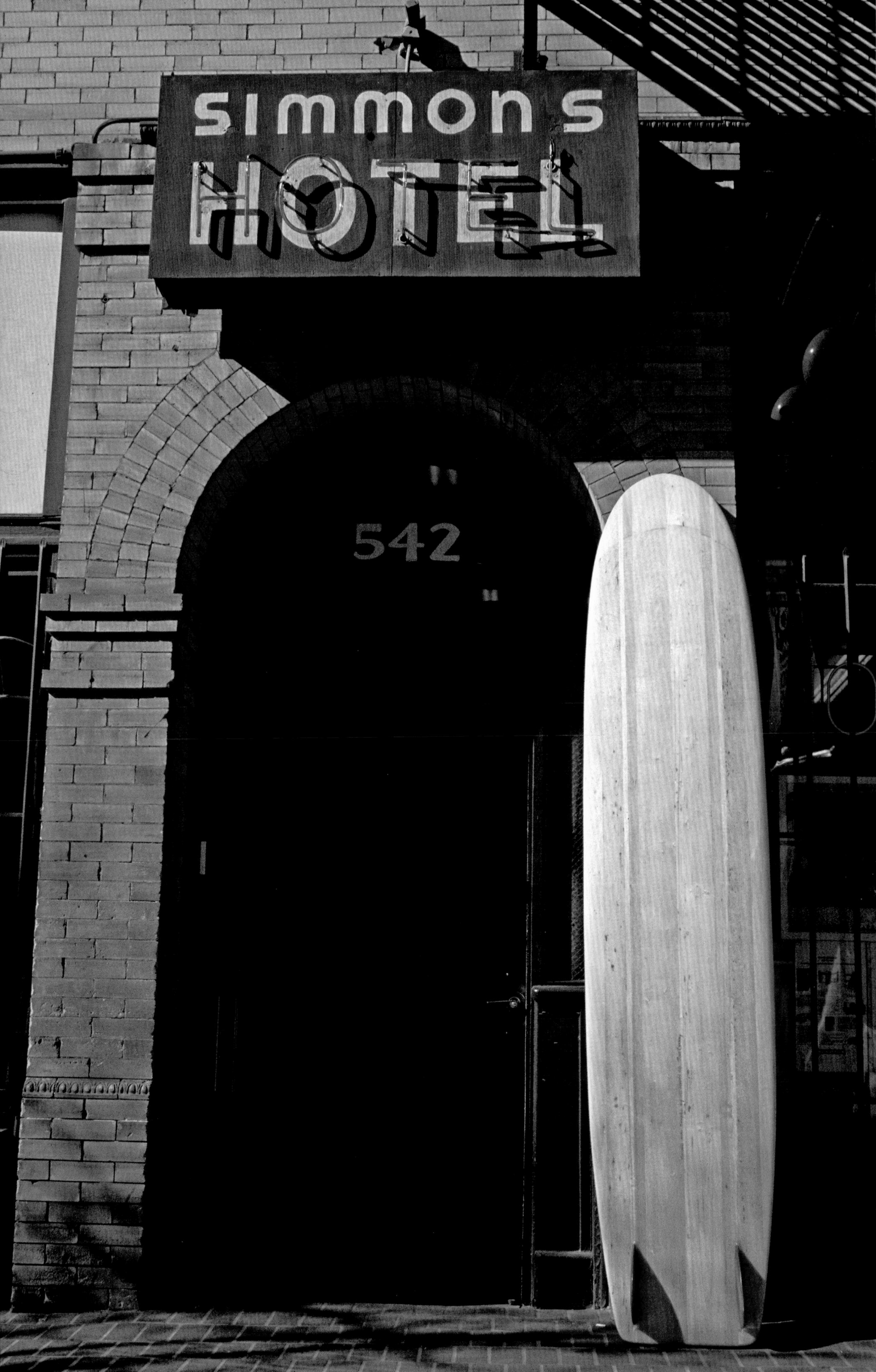
SIMMONS
HOTEL
542

Plates 1–7
Traditional Hawaiian Surfboards:
Papa He'e Nalu Replicas by
Tom "Pohaku" Stone

Tom "Pohaku" Stone is one of the most gifted Hawaiian surfers of his generation. He was a standout during the golden era of Hawaiian single-fin surfing, alongside Reno Abellira, Barry Kanaiaupuni, Jimmy Lucas, Eddie and Clyde Aikau, Gerry Lopez, and Clement "Tiger" Espere. By 1971, Stone had appeared on the cover of *Surfer* magazine and in *Pacific Vibrations*, John Severson's legendary counterculture surf documentary (1970). Stone was a surf star. But as the 1980s bled into the 1990s, he became increasingly disillusioned with the commercialized world of modern surfing. As a native Hawaiian, he felt displaced and alienated by a surf culture that was connected to Wall Street but disconnected from its origins. In 1994, with encouragement from his wife, Anne, he began a formal education to learn the roots of his culture.

Today, Stone holds a bachelor's degree in Hawaiian studies and a master's degree in Pacific Island studies from the University of Hawai'i at Manoa. "I'm into the origins of things, native things," he says. "I heard the *kāhea kahiko*, the old call, and I stopped denying my culture. I started wanting to rediscover the old ways." The boards shown here are recent manifestations of his decades-long anthropological study of native Hawaiian culture. Creating and riding traditional surf craft (and other native craft, such as *hōlua* sleds, used for grassy slopes) has been an important facet of Stone's research. He has conducted hands-on educational programs for the Smithsonian Museum and other institutions around the world. Educating others about the true roots of surfing is a central focus of his life.

The seven surfboards, or *papa he'e nalu*, depicted here are part of a much larger group that Stone is in the process of making with assistance from wooden surfboard aficionado Larry Fuller. The master group consists of thirty boards representing every known design used in traditional Hawaiian surfing, from the massive *olo*, to the wide, stable, buoyant *kīko'o*, to the thin, dynamic *alaia*.

Behind each design group lies a spiritual tradition that goes far beyond the scope of Western labels and performance classifications. Through ritual and ceremony, the

living spirits of
to bring forth
the wood. Eac
of the spirit wo
with, and is gu
tual realm thro
and riding a bo

In the cont
lution, the boa
ancient precur
designs. They
ing designs tha
in the curl, whe
ing, or standing
surfers, who
surfboards, th
They barely flo
they seemed i
Thanks to the
and a few othe
have broken t
tion, and finle
and fly across t
around the wo

Today, as
gresses, plan
on more of the

traditional designs. One example would be the relatively wide leading edge and stern bracketing the parallel running lines found in the latest high-performance boards. The engineering of flex into boards would be another. This is a testament to the hydrodynamics knowingly used by the Hawaiians for centuries. In many ways, modern board designers are only beginning to discover the secrets that have been hiding in plain sight in these ancient designs.

TOM "POHAKU" STONE

Traditional Hawaiian uma, *used as a bellyboard*

2013; 28.75" × 10.75" × .5"; Walnut

COLLECTION OF LARRY FULLER

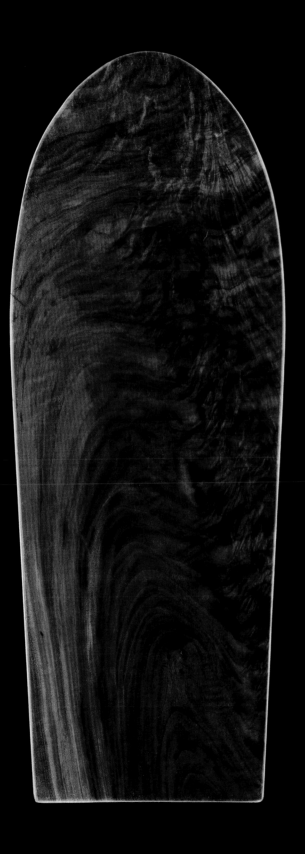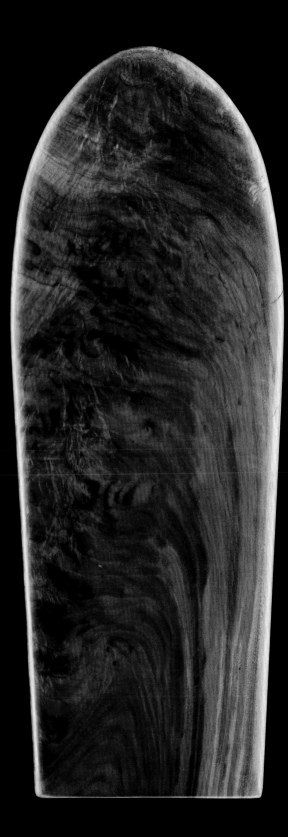

TOM "POHAKU" STONE

Traditional Hawaiian omo, *used as a bellyboard or kneeboard*

2013; 58.5" × 23" × 1.25"; Redwood

COLLECTION OF LARRY FULLER

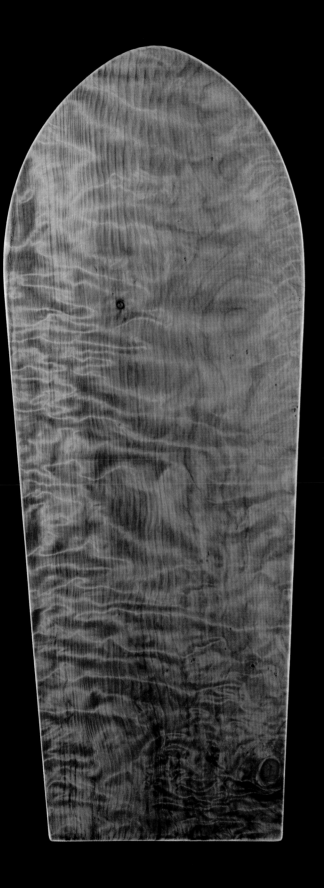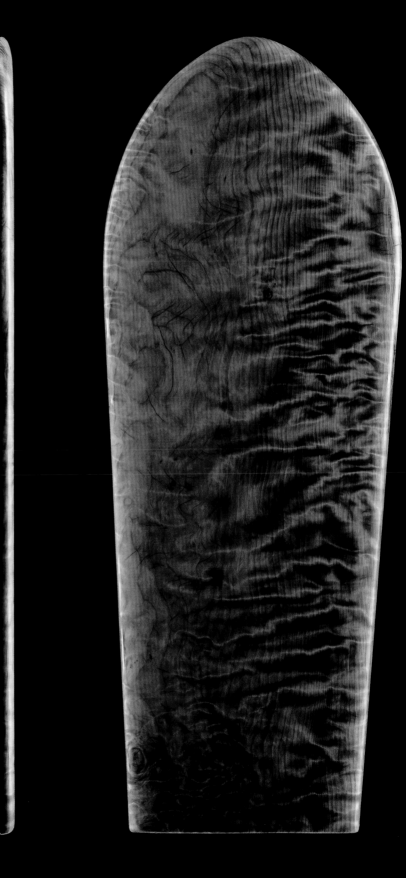

TOM "POHAKU" STONE

Traditional Hawaiian paha, *used as a bellyboard or kneeboard;*
this design became known as a "paipo" *board in the twentieth century*

2013; 47" × 20.5" × 1.15"; 2,700-year-old Sequoia (nontraditional)

COLLECTION OF LARRY FULLER

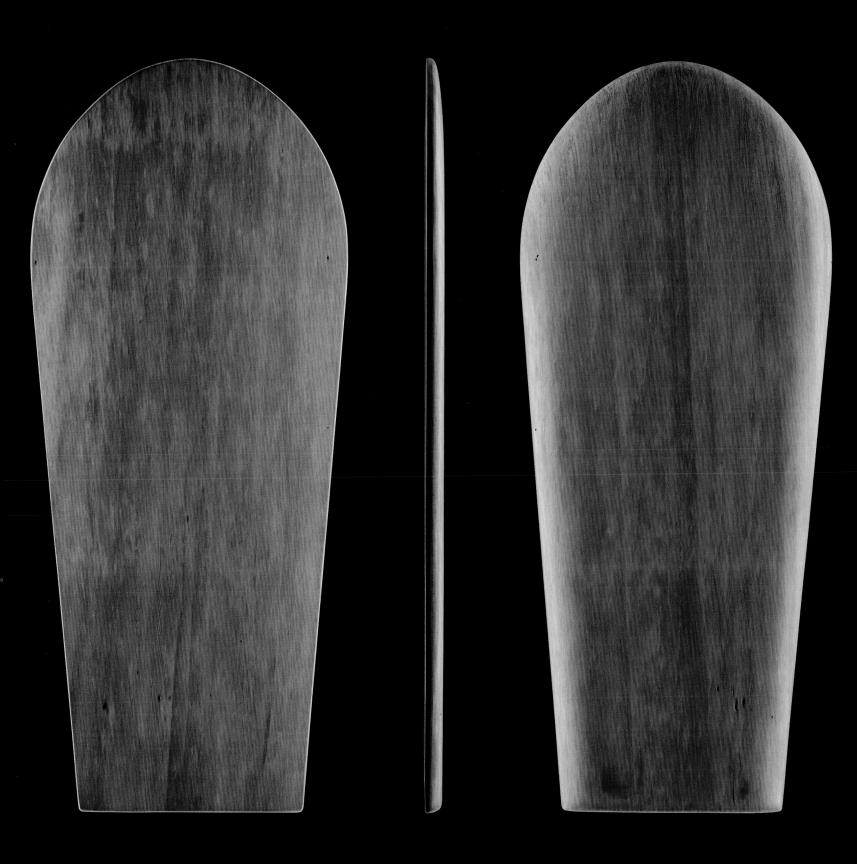

TOM "POHAKU" STONE

Traditional Hawaiian ʻōnini, used as a bellyboard, kneeboard, and stand-up board

2013; 60" × 14.75" × .75"; Redwood

COLLECTION OF LARRY FULLER

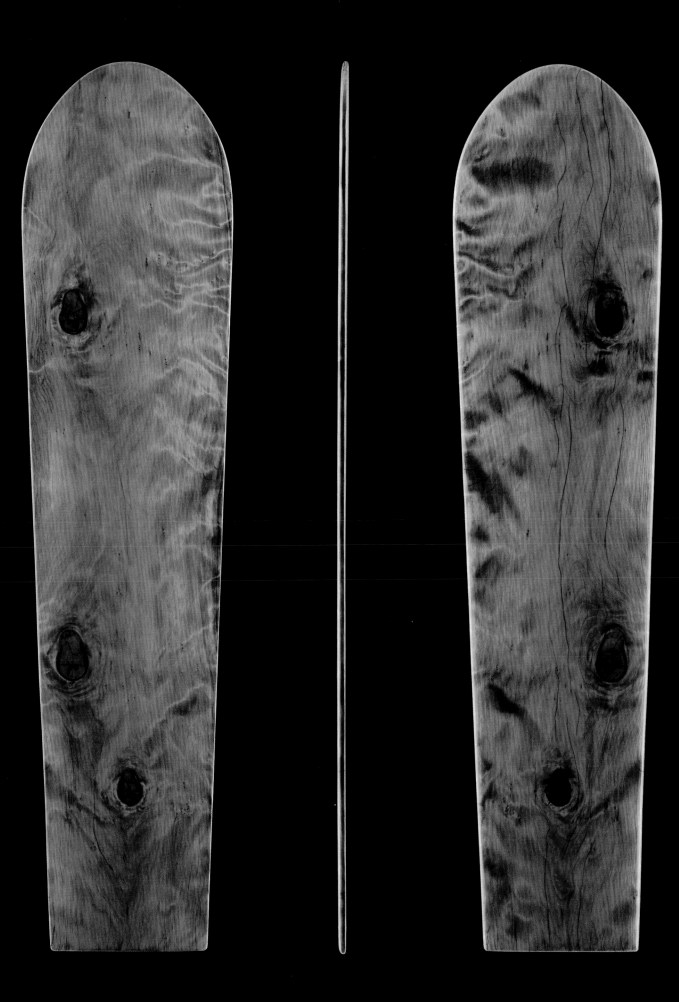

TOM "POHAKU" STONE

*Traditional Hawaiian alaia, used as a bellyboard, kneeboard,
and stand-up board*

2013; 87.5" × 19.5" × .75"; Redwood

COLLECTION OF LARRY FULLER

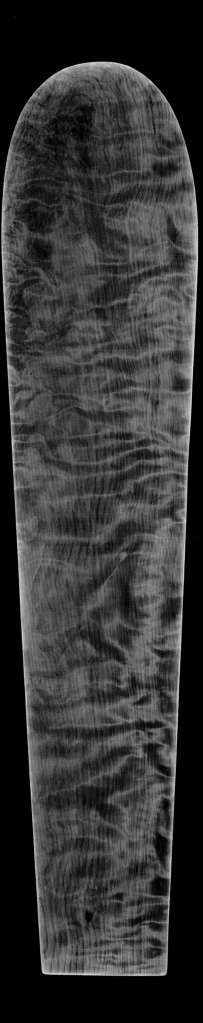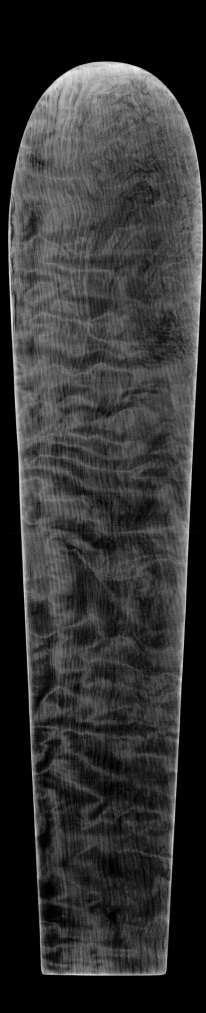

TOM "POHAKU" STONE

Traditional Hawaiian kīoe, used as a stand-up board in critical surf

2013; 96" × 16" × 1"; Walnut (nontraditional)

COLLECTION OF LARRY FULLER

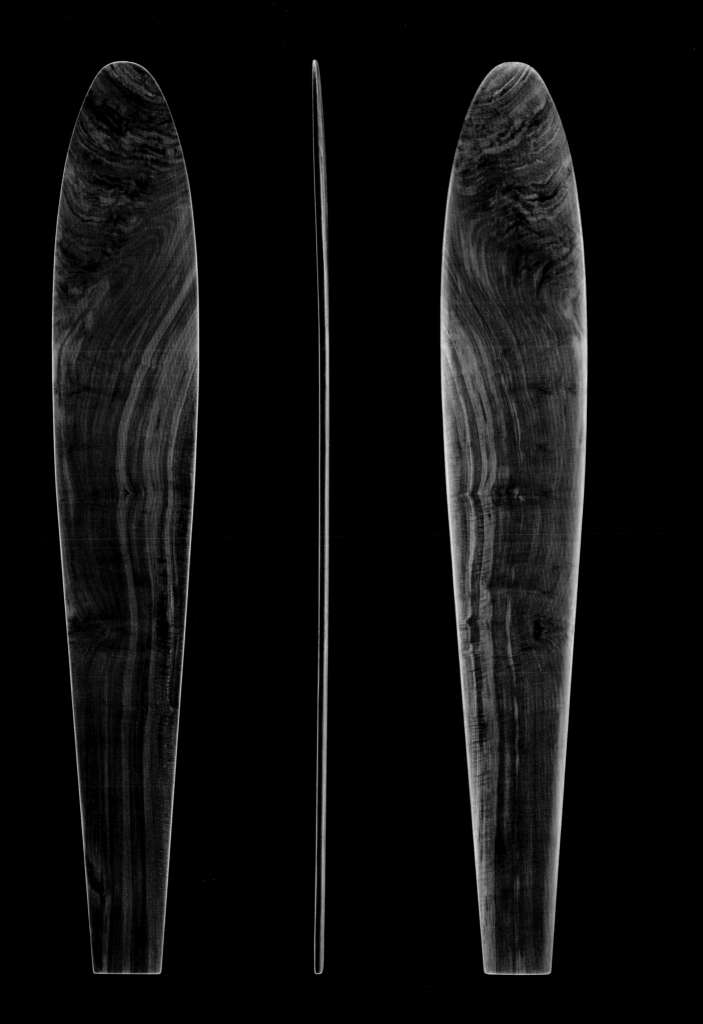

TOM "POHAKU" STONE

Traditional Hawaiian puua, *used as a kneeboard and stand-up board*

2013; 123" × 18.5" × .75"; Redwood

COLLECTION OF LARRY FULLER

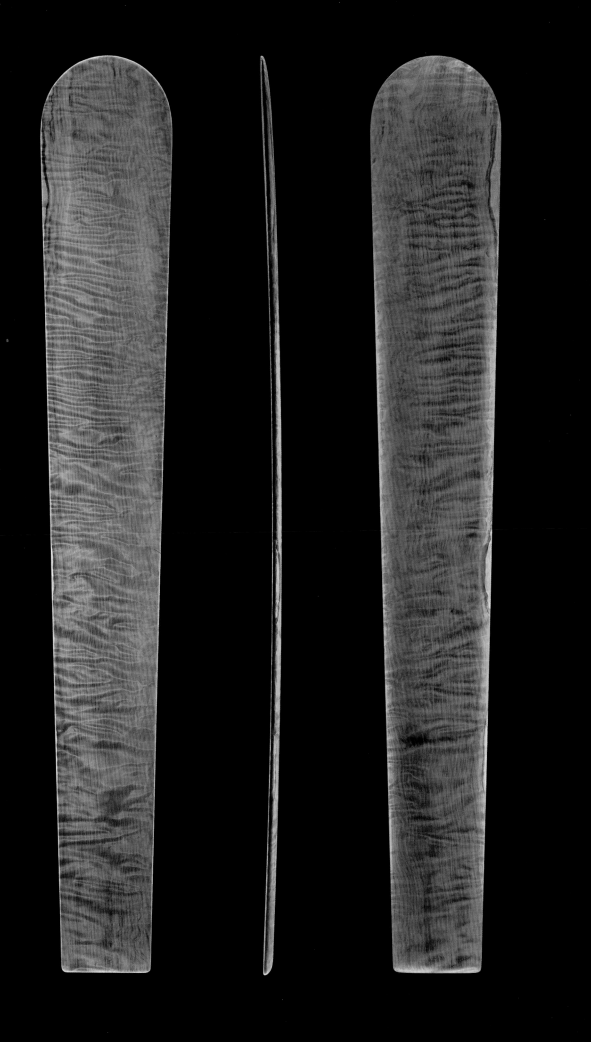

Plates 8–9
Surf-Bathing Bellyboards,
Early Twentieth Century

58| These short boards from the revival era were ridden prone. They sport interesting plan shapes and design features like split tails, side cuts, parallel running lines, and asymmetry. But the post-revival disconnect from the riding styles of the past prevented them from fulfilling their design potential as stand-up boards. Instead, they provided bellyboard thrills aplenty to summer beach goers.

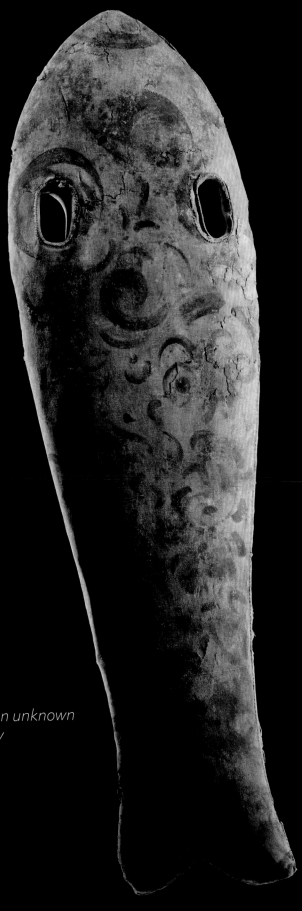

UNKNOWN

Surf-bathing board, used as a bellyboard by tourists at an unknown U.S. mainland resort at the turn of the twentieth century

around 1900; 61" × 17.5" × 2"; Balsa, canvas, paint

PRIVATE COLLECTION

UNKNOWN

'Ōnini-type surf-bathing board, used as a bellyboard

early 20th century; 48"; Redwood

SURFING HERITAGE & CULTURE CENTER

The modern era of surfing is defined by the use of fins, or directional stabilizers. Tom Blake and Woodbridge "Woody" Brown pioneered the use of small, single-keel fins in the 1930s, but it was not until the late 1940s that fins really began to change how surfboards were designed and ridden. The practical application of postwar materials, especially resin and fiberglass, accelerated the use and evolution of finned surfboards. Bob Simmons and Joe Quigg in California and George Downing in Hawai'i were at the forefront of laminated finned designs. Others soon followed, including Bob Sheppard, Dale Velzy, Pat Curren, Al Nelson, and Mike Diffenderfer. Over time, these early finned boards would evolve into the boards that most people ride today.

In Hawai'i, the single fin evolved, through Downing and his cohorts, from the hot curl. The finless hot curl, with its sleek lines, was a perfect single-fin candidate. Adding a fin to the hot curl allowed for a flatter, faster planing bottom and more hydrodynamic rails to replace the deep vee and rolled rails of the original finless versions. Downing and the hot curlers pioneered designing and riding these new single-fin "guns" in huge Hawaiian surf in the 1940s and early 1950s. These boards laid the foundation for a hot curl–derived progression of single fins that evolved into guns, semiguns, and pocket rockets. After decades of refinement in Hawai'i and elsewhere, these boards became much lighter, with better fin templates, rails, rockers, and curves. Surfers like Barry Kanaiaupuni and "Buttons" Kaluhiokalani beautifully realized the Hawaiian-style single fin's performance capabilities in Hawaiian surf in the 1970s.

In California in the late 1930s, single fins initially appeared on wide-tailed planks, and a little later, on early wide-tailed balsa boards. Bob Simmons made many of these wide-tailed balsa single fins, though from 1947 onward, all of his personal boards were dual-keel hydrodynamic planing hulls. Simmons played an enigmatic role in the early single-fin era that has led to a great deal of confusion about his legacy. Though he clearly illustrated that the surfboard of the future would ride rail to rail on outboard fins, he also made single fins—lots of them. The dual-keel planing hull he reserved only for himself and a handful of others. The Simmons single fin was known as the Simmons "spoon." It had a single-keel fin set in the middle of a very wide tail. This caused some major performance issues. Part of the problem was that the early fins had a low aspect ratio, with wide bases and shallow depth. This type of fin needed to be close to the rail in order to work properly. By comparison, the hot curl plan shape, with its narrow tail, worked well as a single fin, because the rails were very close to the fin on each side. But on a wide-tailed Simmons spoon, the rails were often over ten inches away from the fin on either side, rendering it almost useless in turns. At any rate, Simmons did not see this as his problem to solve, as his personal boards had dual fins, one on each rail.

Just after World War II, Joe Quigg addressed some of the issues facing the early wide-tailed single fins in California. He had met the hot curlers in Hawai'i, and he was very receptive to their design concepts and awed by their surfing. Back in California, Quigg pulled in the tail of his boards and used hydrodynamic rails (designed by Simmons), combined with a sophisticated rocker. This greatly improved single-fin performance for California surf. Quigg's Malibu chip boards are a milestone in California single-fin design, and many of the coast's best surfers rode them, including Leslie Williams at Malibu and Robert "Bobby" Patterson and Buzzy Bent at Windansea. In the early 1950s, Windansea surfers Pat Curren, Al Nelson, and Mike Diffenderfer built on the innovations of Quigg in California and Downing and the hot curlers in Hawai'i. Curren and crew took extended trips to the islands, rode huge waves, and helped contribute to the refinement and progression of single-fin boards, especially for big Hawaiian surf.

By any measure, the single-finned, wide-tailed Simmons spoon is an inferior design compared to Quigg's Malibu chip or the Hawaiian single fins born of the hot curl. That being said, by simply removing the center fin and adding two fins on the rail, the major design flaw of the single-fin Simmons spoon

can be remedied. Through one simple modification, an inefficient wide-tailed single fin is transformed into a highly functional hydrodynamic planing hull. In a nutshell, this is exactly what happened two decades later when Mark Richards and Simon Anderson brought outboard fins back into mainstream board design in the late 1970s and early 1980s.

Anderson's three-finned thruster design is the most popular and versatile surfboard ever made. The fins on the thruster, and their function in relation to the rest of the board, can be traced to the pioneering efforts of Simmons, Quigg, Downing, and their peers. Quigg's Malibu chip and Downing's early gun shapes (both of which are single-fin designs) mark the earliest beginnings of the thruster's rockers, curves, and trailing fin. Simmons's dual-keel planing hull is the origin of its outboard fins, rails, wetted planing surface, and dynamic rail-to-rail capabilities. Anderson did not kill the single fin or the Simmons planing hull; he brought them together and kept them alive.

BOB SIMMONS

Simmons spoon single fin

mid- to late 1940s; 114" × 23" × 3.5"; Balsa, resin, fiberglass, varnish
(only the spoon nose is glassed; the rest of the board is varnished)

COLLECTION OF ERIC "BIRD" HUFFMAN

UNKNOWN

Malibu chip, probably made for a young boy or girl

1950s; 61" × 18.75"; Balsa scraps, resin, fiberglass

SURFING HERITAGE & CULTURE CENTER

HANS NEWMAN

Kneeboard with wings

1972; 62" × 19.25" × 2.75"; Polyurethane foam, resin, fiberglass

COLLECTION OF HANS NEWMAN

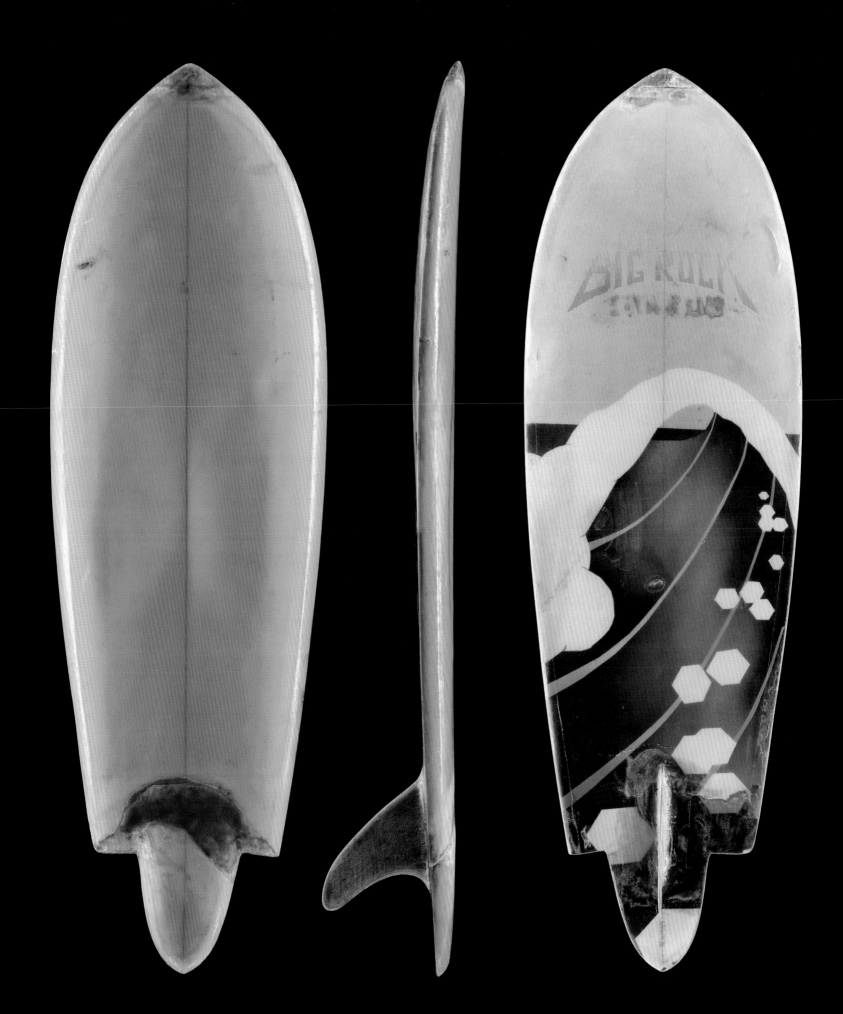

In order to understand the unique role that Bob Simmons played in the craft and design of surfboards, one must first acknowledge the accomplishments and influence of his nonsurfing older brother, Edward "Dewey" Simmons. Dewey was an electrical engineer who earned a master's degree in science at the California Institute of Technology in 1936. He continued to work at Caltech after receiving his degree, and in 1938, he invented the bonded wire resistance electric strain gauge. The Simmons strain gauge revolutionized engineering and industrial design by providing an accurate and unprecedented means of measuring structural stress on everything from aircraft to boat hulls to bridges. The venerable Franklin Institute in Philadelphia awarded the Edward Longstreth Medal to Dewey in 1944, and in 1949, he received a U.S. patent for his invention. Dewey went on to design sophisticated radar systems during World War II, and he worked on other classified projects for the U.S. government.

Dewey's strain gauge was immediately put to use by aerospace engineers and naval architects. It was a crucial tool used for gathering data that was eventually published in postwar scientific texts. Among these published studies (many of which remain standards in their respective fields) are two that guided and affirmed Bob Simmons as he designed the blueprint for today's multifinned surfboards. These texts are *Naval Architecture of Planing Hulls* by Lindsay Lord (1946) and *The Theory of Wing Sections* by Ira H. Abbot (1949).

Bob Simmons had a mind that was every bit as formidable as his elder brother's, and he quickly followed Dewey to Caltech. There he studied mathematics and engineering on scholarship. As a teenager, Bob devoured everything of scientific and mathematical interest that Dewey brought home. He spent hours in the garage watching Dewey perform experiments that would eventually lead to the invention of the strain gauge. For most of his short life, Bob was immersed in science and mathematics at an extraordinarily high level. From the time he started surfing in 1939 until his death in 1954, he tapped directly into the scientific world of wartime and postwar Southern California. He was not just some bohemian surfer crackpot snooping around boat shops looking for resin and fiberglass; he was a mathematician and scientist with deep ties to Caltech, Librascope, the Scripps Institution of Oceanography, and Douglas Aircraft, where he worked first as a machinist and then as a mathematician. Given his intellect, he had unrestricted access to a wealth of relevant new information and new materials. His passion for surfing and his practical skill as a craftsman came together to form a thoroughly modern surfboard design: the hydrodynamic planing hull.

If Ray and Charles Eames had designed surfboards in Los Angeles during the 1940s instead of furniture, chances are they would have come up with something a lot like the Simmons planing hull. The aerodynamically inspired organic curves found in their plywood and fiberglass chairs were conceived and prototyped at the same time and in the same Los Angeles neighborhoods as Simmons's surfboards. They probably used the same suppliers, like General Veneer, for materials such as plywood, and they shared the same employers, like Douglas Aircraft, where

Simmons and the Eameses both worked in 1952. But while aesthetics played a big part in the look of Eames furniture and other California modern design, the Simmons surfboards used aeronautical curves and materials purely for function. The Simmons planing hull was not trying to *look* like an aerodynamic design; it *functioned* as an aerodynamic design.

While others dreamed of boards shaped like rocket ships, darts, javelins, and spears, all in the name of speed, Simmons quietly arrived at the truth of the matter through mathematical calculation. He analyzed the physics and forces of ocean waves, the weight and mass of the human body, the deflection of kinetic energy by the rails, and a multitude of other factors. The resulting design appeared (and still appears) counterintuitive. Speed came not from pointy noses and tails but from width. Rails didn't just "bite" and "hold"; they also lifted. Fin design and placement was determined not by the shape of the tail or the plan shape, but by water flow off the hull and the rails. Planing speed was governed by one set of principles found in *Naval Architecture of Planing Hulls*, rails, fins, and turning by

another set of principles found in *The Theory of Wing Sections*. For Simmons, nothing distorted and compromised the basic function of the hydrodynamic planing hull so much as the use of a single fin.

By 1947, Simmons had defined the relationship between rails, fins, and planing surface, as used in today's high-performance multifinned boards. The rail was essentially an airfoil, like an airplane wing, designed to lift. The main purpose of the fin was to keep the lifting rail anchored in the wave face, directing and controlling its speed. The most efficient and dynamic way to increase the holding power of the fin while exploiting the energy created by lift and planing was to place the fin as close to the rail as possible. A wide planing surface fore and aft further increased speed. For Simmons, planing hull science dictated that the stern of the surfboard, where the outboard fins were placed, be at least ten inches wide. Therefore, he began using two fins, one on each rail. This method is prolific today, in all sizes of surf, but it would

not enter into mainstream design until more than twenty years after his death. The genesis of modern multifinned rail-to-rail surfing is the Simmons hydrodynamic planing hull.

Today, the fundamental principles defined by Simmons in the planing hull are being knowingly applied to a new generation of surfboards. The original planing hulls made by Simmons in the 1940s and 1950s were often monolithic in scale. Australian shaper Daniel Thomson recently discovered that the originals could be scaled down within their original proportions by using a specific aspect ratio already present in vintage Simmons boards. Thomson's shorter, narrower board is the "modern planing hull," which is perhaps the best high-performance surfboard yet designed. Though touted as "the surfboard of the future," it is deeply grounded in Simmons's pioneering work from the 1940s.

BOB SIMMONS

Hydrodynamic planing hull with dual keels

1949; 122" × 24" × 4"; "Sandwich" veneer laminate construction, marine plywood deck, balsa rails and bottom, foam core, redwood keels, resin, fiberglass

SURFING HERITAGE *&* **CULTURE CENTER**

BOB SIMMONS

Hydrodynamic planing hull with concave bottom and dual keels

1949; 122" × 23.5" × 3.5"; Balsa, redwood, resin, fiberglass

SURFING HERITAGE & CULTURE CENTER

BOB SIMMONS

Hydrodynamic planing hull with slots and dual keels

early 1950s; 96" × 23" × 3.5"; Balsa, resin, fiberglass

COLLECTION OF MEISTRELL FAMILY

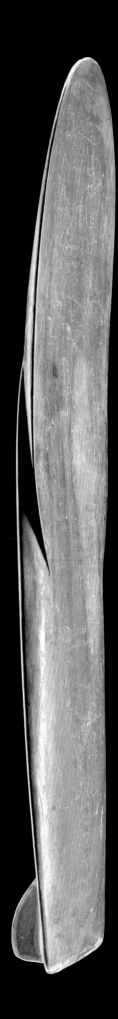

BOB SIMMONS, MODIFIED BY UNKNOWN

Reshaped Simmons board with dual keels

early 1950s; 94" × 23" × 3"; Balsa, redwood keels, resin, fiberglass
(the nose scarf shows evidence that this was originally a longer
board that was reshaped with a "pulled" nose)

HISCHIER FAMILY COLLECTION

Hydrodynamic planing hull with dual keels

1950, restored in 2001; 108" × 23" × 3"; Balsa, redwood keels, resin, fiberglass (Simmons built this board custom for John Elwell and Margie Manoch. It was made near Dempsey Holder's lifeguard station in Imperial Beach, California. It was originally a single fin, but Simmons later instructed Elwell on making and applying dual fins.)

COLLECTION OF JOHN ELWELL

The *paipo* is a twentieth-century incarnation of the traditional *paha* board. Some *paipo* boards were made from traditional native woods like *koa*; others were built from the urban detritus of Honolulu's concrete jungle. Home-built *paipo* boards were (and still are) an integral facet of local wave-riding culture in Hawai'i. No two were exactly alike, as riders customized the boards to suit their individual preferences. Sometimes existing items like old wooden ironing boards, real estate signs, and plastic fast-food trays were repurposed as *paipo* boards. Just about anything that offered a planing surface and did not sink like a stone was fair game.

Like the ancestral *paha*, *paipo* boards were thin, with little buoyancy. Without the crutch of floatation, the *paipo*, by necessity, maximized lift and planing. It makes sense, then, that many *paipo* boards have an aspect ratio very close to that of Lindsay Lord's A6 planing plate, the fastest and most efficient shape in his 1946 study, *Naval Architecture of Planing Hulls*. Since Lord worked with local people and conducted his study in Honolulu, it seems likely (though unconfirmed) by, the *paipo* riders and their simple, yet incredibly fast planing craft.

The *paipo* went through its own design progression in the twentieth century. In the 1950s and 1960s, Wally Froiseth and Val Valentine began building *paipo* boards on a very small commercial scale, using innovative design and construction processes. In California, Dave Sweet and Phil Edwards dabbled in production bellyboard design, with an eye toward making a user-friendly beach toy for the untapped and potentially lucrative non-surfing summer beach market. As surfing spread in the 1960s, finned foam and fiberglass bellyboards and kneeboards made by branded surfboard manufacturers appeared in surf shops in Hawai'i and on the mainland. These production boards were often labeled and marketed as "*paipos*," though their buoyancy, rigidity, and thickness were hardly compatible with true *paipo* design.

In the 1970s, Tom Morey introduced the boogie board. With a plan shape identical to that of Lord's A6 planing plate, the boogie board was soft, flexible, buoyant, and extremely functional. Morey hit the marketing nail on the head, and the boogie board went on to become the most widely ridden surf craft in history. Most Hawaiian *paipo* riders jumped on boogie boards (with spectacular results), and by the late 1970s, the home-made, handcrafted *paipo* had all but vanished from the islands.

But a few individuals scattered throughout Hawai'i continued to build and ride *paipo* boards, and today the boards are enjoying something of a revival. Examples include the high-tech and hydrodynamically sophisticated *paipo* boards built and designed by Paul Lindbergh and ridden by Sean Ross, whose *paipo* riding in huge Hawaiian surf is legendary. Lindbergh's boards have been evolving for forty-eight years, with design input from Ross. Their point of origin is a high school woodshop class in 1965. Another example is Valentine Ching, who mastered stand-up *paipo* riding in the late 1950s. In recent years, Ching has passed on his knowledge to a younger generation, including Tom Henry, who picked up where Ching left off, standing on a 3'9" piece of plywood.

The influence of the *paipo* on shortboard surfing and board design in the twentieth century is undeniable. The *paipo* maintained a link to ancient boards and riding styles while demonstrating, in the midst of the longboard era, that incredible things were possible on thin, wide, flexible boards with little floatation. Whether ridden prone, like Ross, or standing, like Wally Froiseth and Valentine Ching, the *paipo* was a testament to the power of pure planing hydrodynamics. The effect the *paipo* had in the early 1960s on young Hawaiians like Reno Abellira, Jeff Ching, and Larry Bertlemann changed the course of surfing forever.

UNKNOWN

Paipo

early 1960s; 47" × 21.5" × 0.5"; Plywood, resin, paint

SURFING HERITAGE & CULTURE CENTER

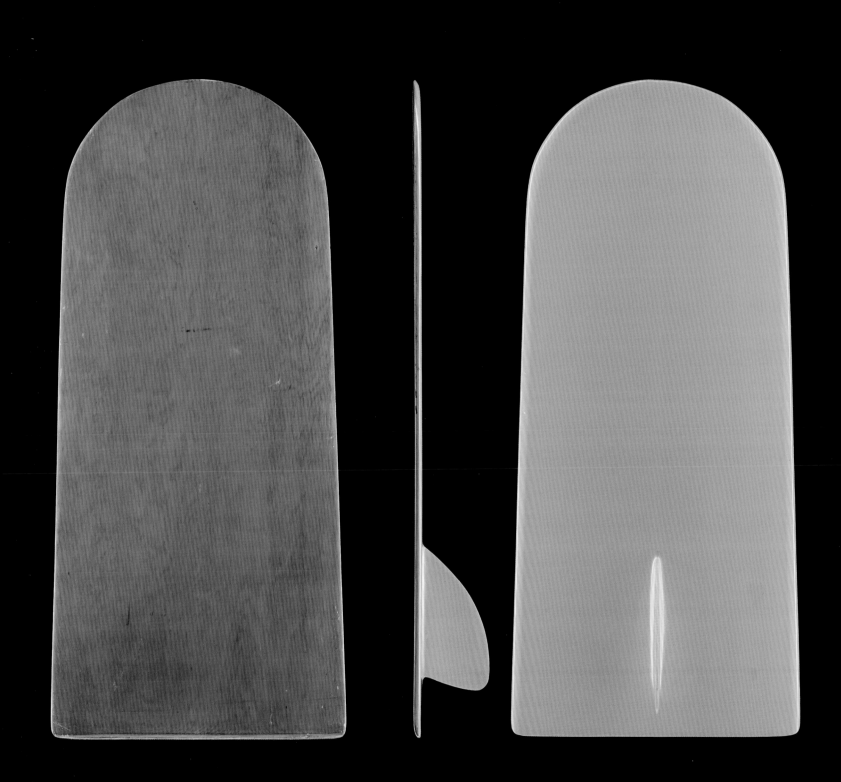

VAL VALENTINE

Paipo nui, *Hawai'i*

1960s; 43" × 30" × .0325"; Laminated plywood veneer

SURFING HERITAGE & CULTURE CENTER

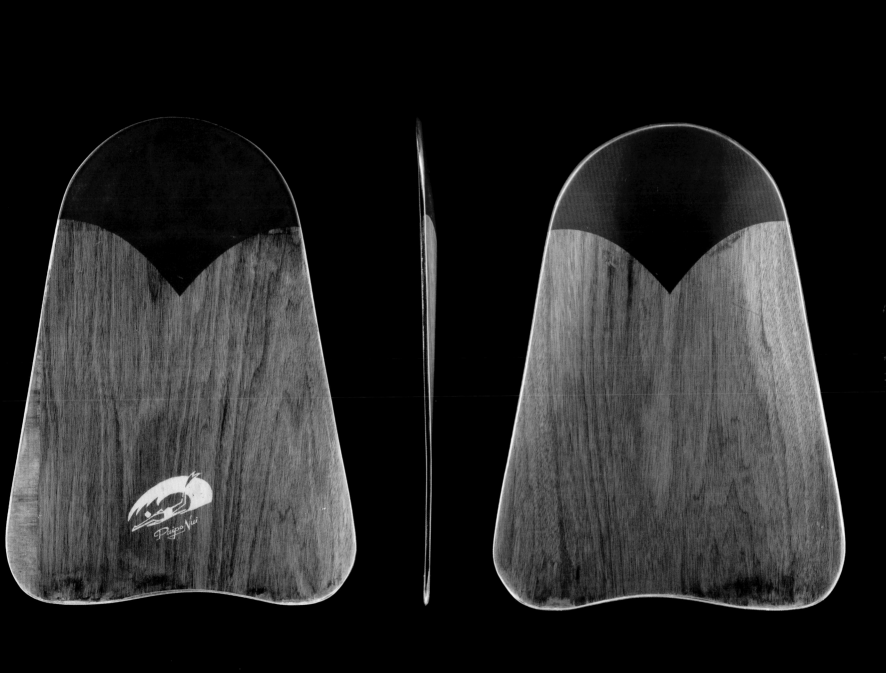

PHIL EDWARDS

Bellyboard plug for mold

date unknown; 43" × 23" × 1.375"; Resin, fiberglass

SURFING HERITAGE & CULTURE CENTER

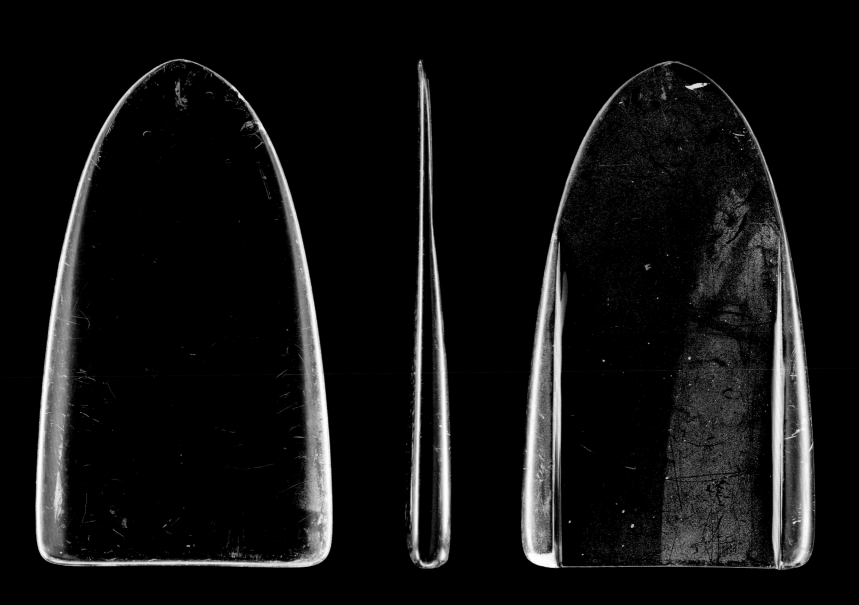

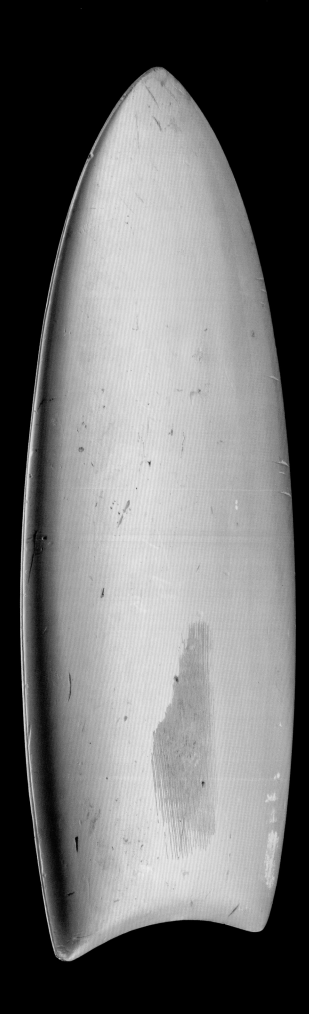

86 |

DAVE SWEET

Foam bellyboard prototype

1950s; 43" × 20" × 2.25"; Polyurethane foam

SURFING HERITAGE & CULTURE CENTER

CHALLENGER

Bellyboard with dual fins

mid-1960s; 44" × 18" × 1.5"; Polyurethane foam,
resin, balsa, redwood, fiberglass, color tint

COLLECTION OF HANS NEWMAN

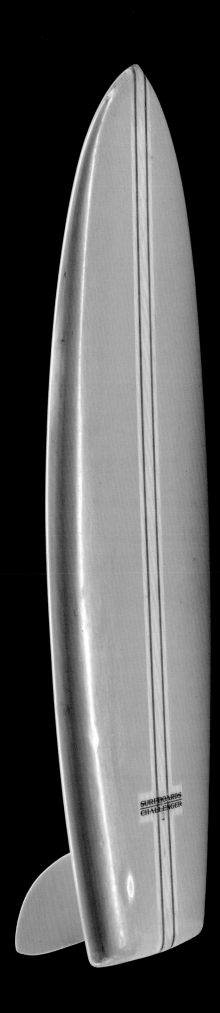

Plate 23
British Bellyboard, 1950s

88 | Though the English have been familiar with
surfing since making contact with the Tahi-
tians in 1767, the earliest-recorded surfing in
Britain was not until 1890. The board shown
here is an example of a beach-bathing bellyboard. It is essentially the same design as the
'ōnini boards of ancient Hawai'i, with some
mild innovation, such as steam-bent camber in the nose. It is a design Captain Cook
and his crew would have seen in use when
they made contact with the Hawaiians over
two centuries ago. Today in England, these
boards are standard equipment at the annual
World Bellyboard Championships in Corn-
wall, a delightfully eccentric British celebration of surfing.

board, used as a bellyboard, England

; Steam-bent marine plywood

AAC

Plate 24
Itago Board, Japan, 1962

90| The *itago* is a surf-bathing bellyboard that was used in Japan. The earliest written account of *itago* riding is from the haiku of a poet from Sakata, who describes watching children riding *itago* boards in 1821. The earliest *itago*, which means "floor board," was removed from a fishing boat. In the late nineteenth century, *itago* riding spread beyond fishing communities to the emerging seaside resort towns along the Japanese coast, where they were used as bellyboards, lifesaving devices, and swimming aids.

The board shown here was made by Haruo Tsukakoshi in 1962 during the twilight of the traditional *itago* era, near the popular surf-bathing resort of Zushi beach. Tsukakoshi made the board for his girlfriend Yoko, who later became his wife.

HARUO TSUKAKOSHI

Itago *surf-bathing board, used as a bellyboard, Japan*

1962; 31" × 13" × .5"; Plywood, paint
COLLECTION OF NOBUHITO "NOBBY" OHKAWA

Plates 25–26
Kneeboards by George Greenough,
1962–1980

George Greenough built the balsa kneeboard spoon shown here in 1962. It originally had dual fins, but Greenough later removed them, replacing them with a single fin. He preferred single fins on his spoon designs ever after. This board is a remarkable example of Greenough's progressive and deeply personal approach to board design. At the height of the longboard era, Greenough was completely off in his own world, getting deep in the tube and carving the face on this tiny kneeboard. The dual-fin experiment, the diamond tail, the knife-sharp edges in the back of the board, and the kneeboard approach itself all bear witness to a design mentality and surfing style that was decades ahead of its time. Greenough's idea of surfing eventually became everyone's idea of surfing, but in 1962, the mainstream and Greenough were in two different universes.

The board shown on page 95 came years later, after Greenough had incorporated flex into his boards, which happened shortly after the 1962 balsa board. "Once I experienced flex," he said, "I never went back." This board has two flexible pintails with fabric stretched between them.

GEORGE GREENOUGH

Kneeboard balsa spoon with single fin

1962; 58" × 19" × 1"; Balsa, resin, fiberglass, metal

HISCHIER FAMILY COLLECTION

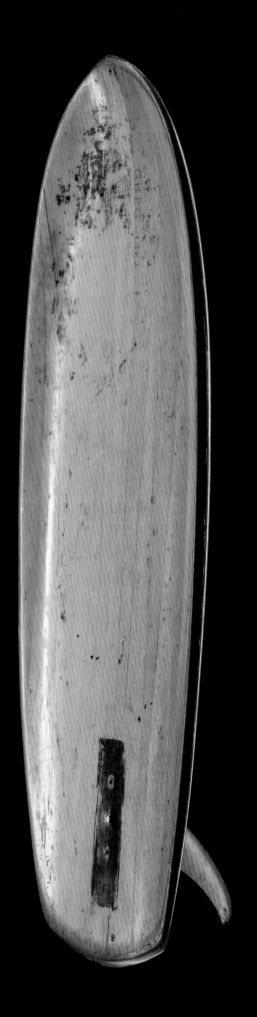

GEORGE GREENOUGH

Kneeboard flex-tail with single fin

1980; 62" × 18" × 1.5"; Polyurethane foam, resin, carbon fiber, fabric

SURFING HERITAGE & CULTURE CENTER

Plate 27
Twin Pin by Nick and Barry Mirandon, 1968

96 | Nick and Barry Mirandon grew up surfing Windansea in the 1950s. In 1957 they watched in amazement as Butch Van Artsdalen rode a 5'6" dual-finned balsa board built by Al Nelson. Ten years later, in 1967, the Greenough-inspired shortboard revolution was spreading from Australia to California via the "V" bottom board popularized by Bob McTavish. The Mirandons welcomed the shortboard concept and drew on their memories of Nelson's board to create perhaps the earliest multifinned stand-up design of the shortboard revolution: the twin pin. The Mirandons' use of a wide, split tail with dual fins helped to motivate and affirm Steve Lis in the early days of the fish.

Today, Nick's son Eli carries on the creative legacy of his father and uncle. A world-class surfer, Eli collaborates with his father, building twenty-first-century versions of the twin pin with extreme side cuts. Eli's ultra-modern surfing on these strange-looking craft would amaze skeptics.

NICK AND BARRY MIRANDON

Twin pin

1968; 96" × 22" × 2.75"; Polyurethane foam, resin, fiberglass

COLLECTION OF HANS NEWMAN

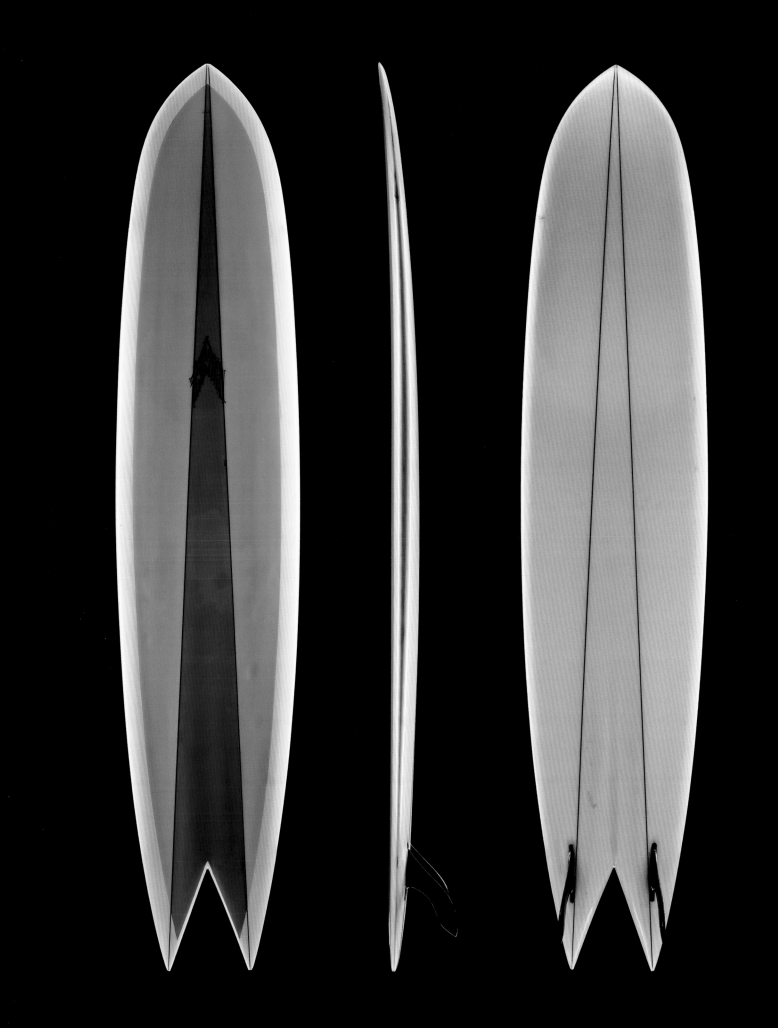

"Pluto Platter" kneeboard flex-tail with single fin

1969; 56"; Polyurethane foam, resin, fiberglass

COLLECTION OF TY PONDER

Plates 28–40
Kneeboards by Terry Hendricks, 1967–2004

98| Terry Hendricks, Ph.D., was a mathematician and physicist. Like Bob Simmons before him, he created surfboards that were material expressions of calculations explored in his mind, in numbers and theory, long before they took physical form. No doubt, in Hendricks's mind, these designs existed in a perfect, fulfilled state. His thoughts took shape and became tangible (if not always comprehensible) in the boards he left behind. Hendricks was a friend of George Greenough and a friend and mentor to Steve Lis and Stanley Pleskunas. One of the boards shown here was made in collaboration with Lis and Pleskunas.

Functional and efficient board design seems to evolve naturally within the constraints of the kneeboard stance. Kneeboarders like Pleskunas, Greenough, and Lis cast aside the hangups found in stand-up boards in favor of the superlative performance of the kneeboard. Their designs are vehicles that reflect, perhaps more than anything else, a desire to gain access to and escape from the most dynamic, powerful, and mysterious places on the wave face. In magnitudes of intensity, the kneeboarder's forays into and out of this zone hit levels that seem to alter consciousness. Flying into and out of the tube and then banking, torquing, and carving on the face makes conventional surfing seem quaint and pedestrian, almost unrelated.

Bob Simmons often rode waves on his knees. The design concepts shared by Simmons, Hendricks, Greenough, and Lis become apparent when their boards are seen grouped together. Though the details sometimes differ, they are all united in principle—a testament to pure, functional hydrodynamics.

Hendricks spent the last decades of his life surfing exclusively at night. His final achievement was the "Fly by Night Pelicanfoil," a bodyboard that used hydrofoils to lift several inches off the surface and "fly" like a pelican across the wave. He rode it successfully, often alone, always at night. There is perhaps no better example of how the hands and mind of a surfer can take him or her to places beyond the imagination.

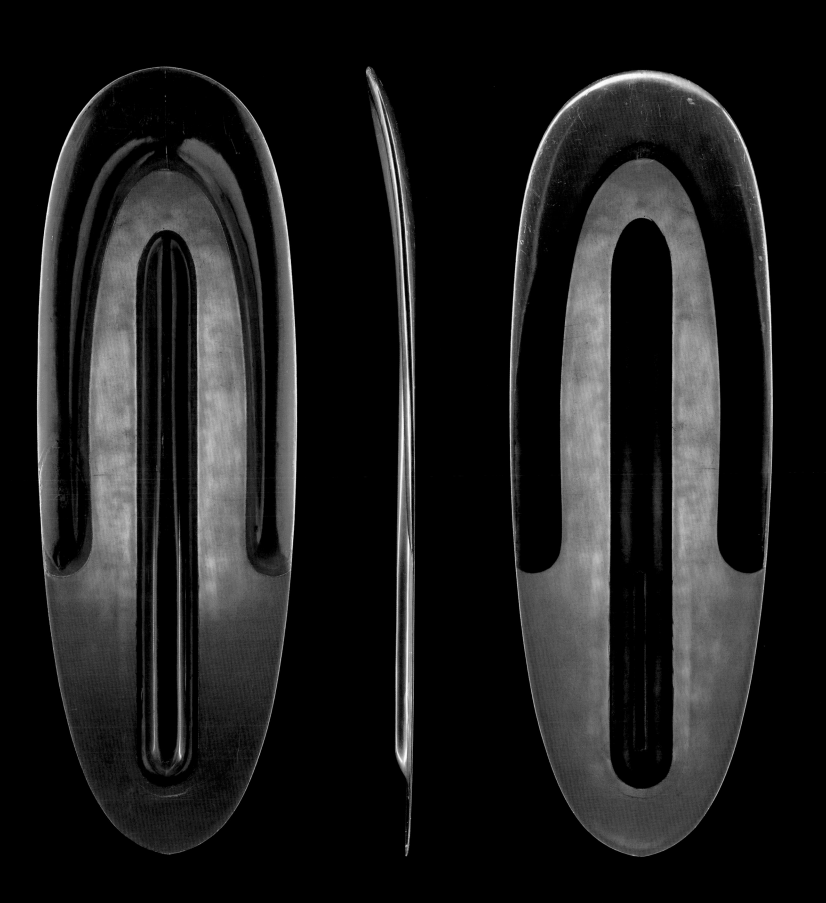

TERRY HENDRICKS

Kneeboard flex-tail, unfinished

1970s; 67.5" × 23" × 1.25"; Polyurethane foam, resin, fiberglass

COLLECTION OF TY PONDER

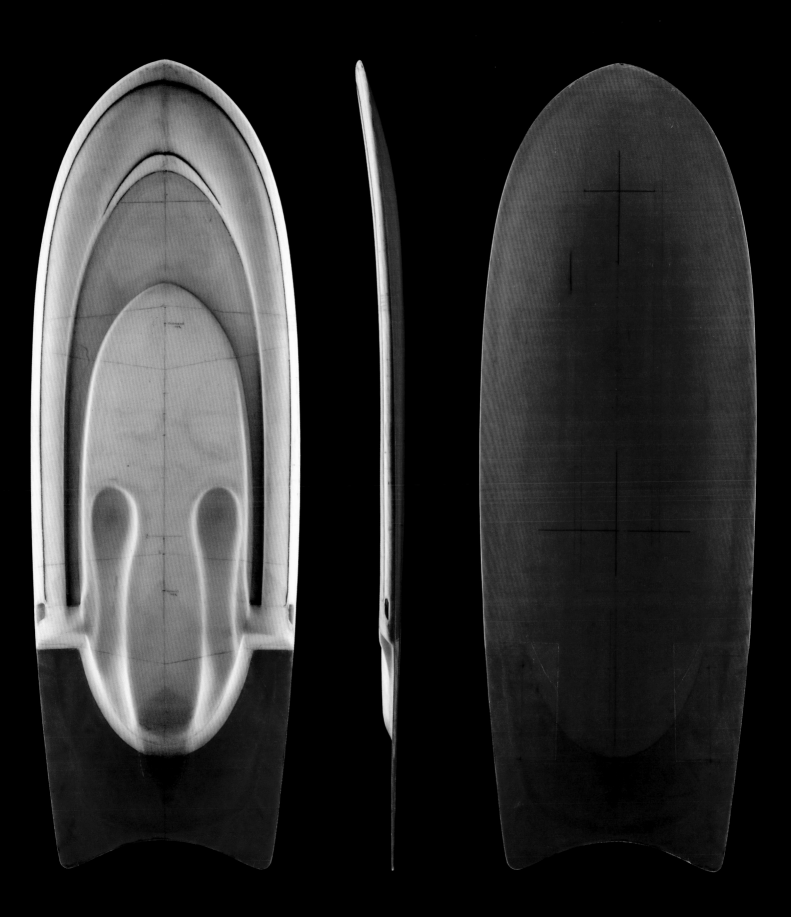

TERRY HENDRICKS

Kneeboard flex-tail with dual fins

early 1970s; 68"; Polyurethane foam, resin, fiberglass

COLLECTION OF TY PONDER

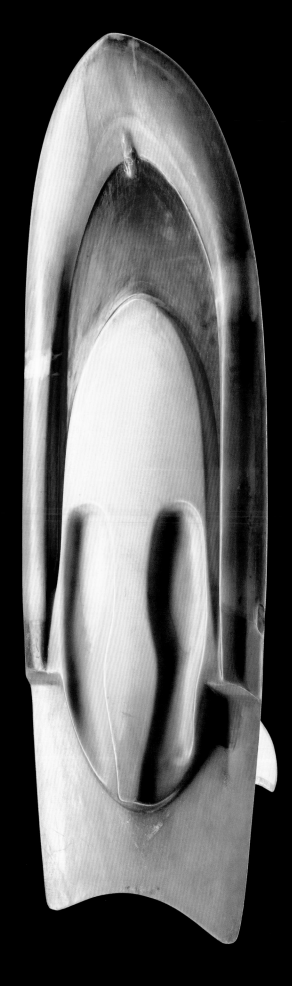

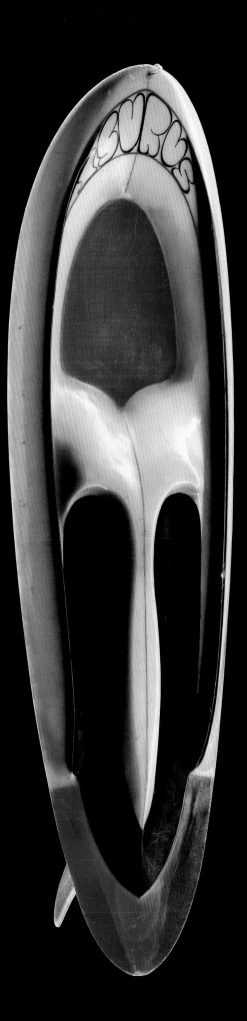

TERRY HENDRICKS | 103

"Isurus" kneeboard flex-tail with single fin

early 1970s; 62"; Polyurethane foam, resin, fiberglass

COLLECTION OF TY PONDER

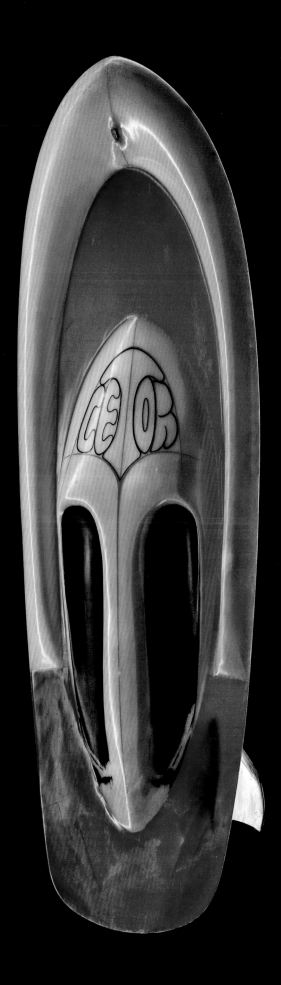

TERRY HENDRICKS

"Cetor" kneeboard flex-tail with dual keels

1970s; 63"; Polyurethane foam, resin, fiberglass

COLLECTION OF TY PONDER

TERRY HENDRICKS

"Pluto Platter" kneeboard spoon flex-tail with single fin

1969; 56" × 18.75" × 1"; Polyurethane foam, resin, fiberglass

COLLECTION OF TY PONDER

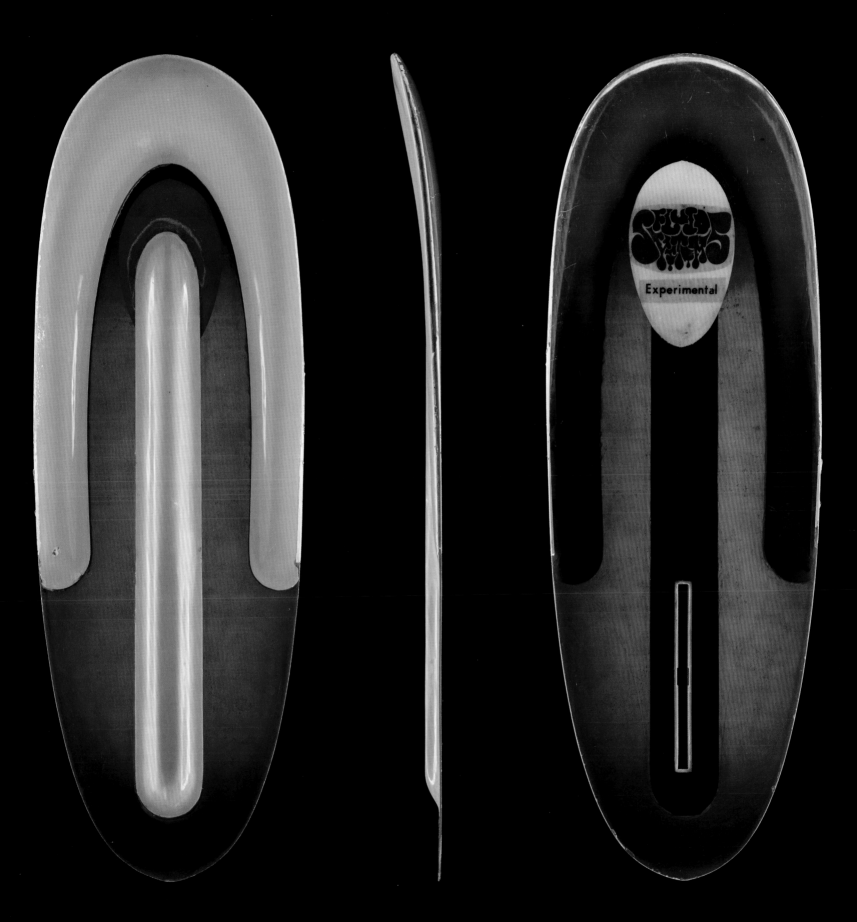

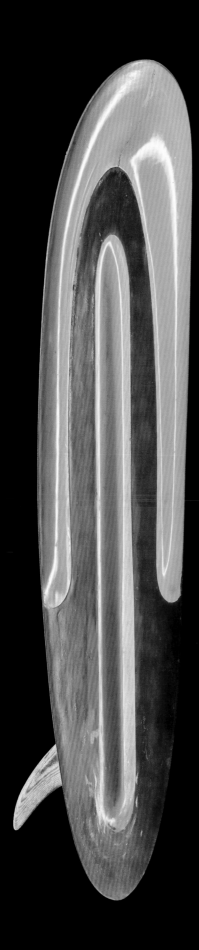

TERRY HENDRICKS

"Pluto Platter" kneeboard spoon flex-tail with single fin

1969; 56" × 20" × 2"; Polyurethane foam, resin, fiberglass

COLLECTION OF ERIC "BIRD" HUFFMAN

TERRY HENDRICKS

Kneeboard with five fin boxes

1990s; 64"; Polyurethane foam, resin, fiberglass

COLLECTION OF TY PONDER

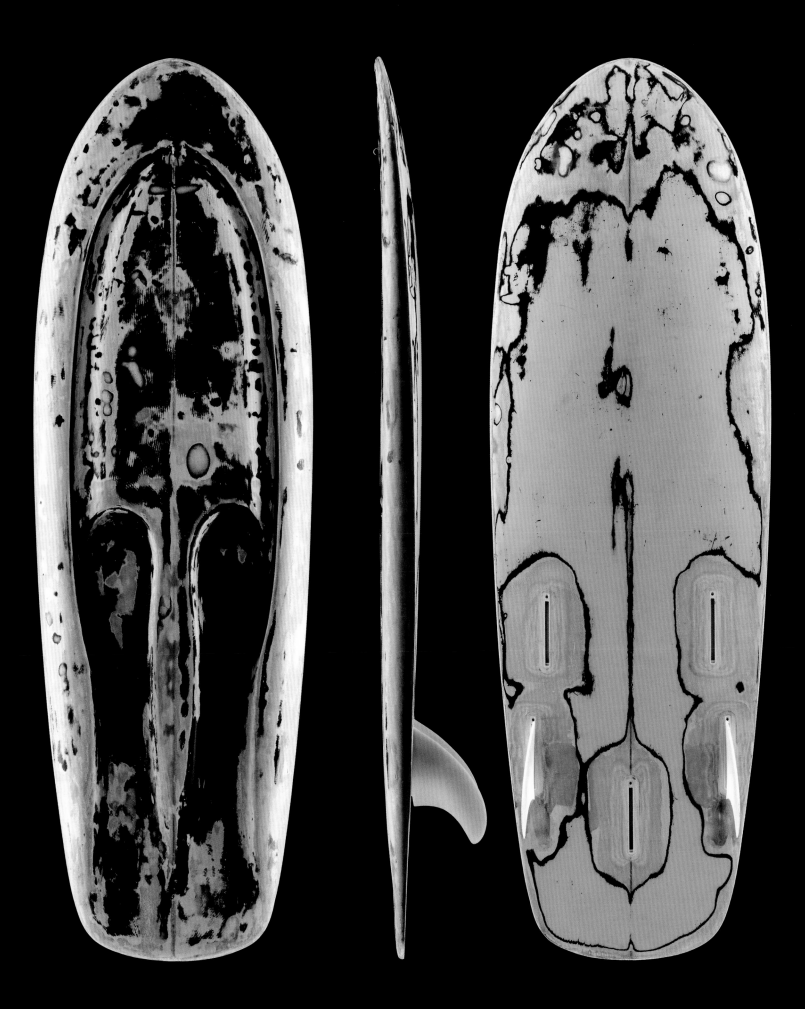

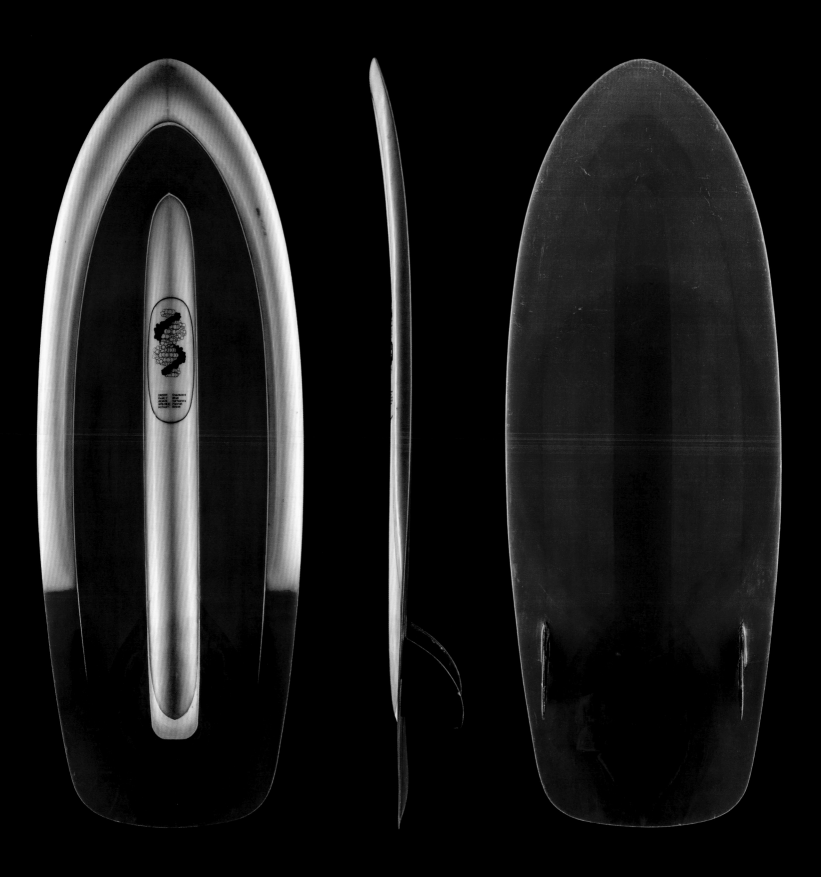

TERRY HENDRICKS

Kneeboard flex-tail with dual fins

1970s; 51.5" × 22" × 1.5"; Polyurethane foam, resin, fiberglass

COLLECTION OF TY PONDER

TERRY HENDRICKS

"Red October" kneeboard flex-tail with dual keels

1996; 69" × 20" × 2.5"; Polyurethane foam, resin, fiberglass

COLLECTION OF TY PONDER

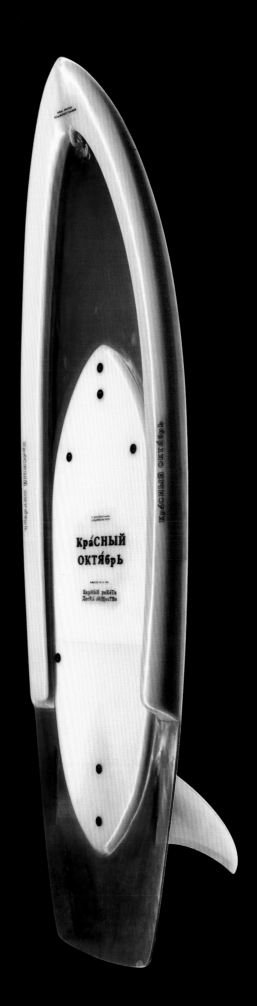

TERRY HENDRICKS

"Cypselurus" laminated foam template for kneeboard

July 4, 1994; 69" × 23.5" × .5"; Polyurethane foam, resin, fiberglass

COLLECTION OF TY PONDER

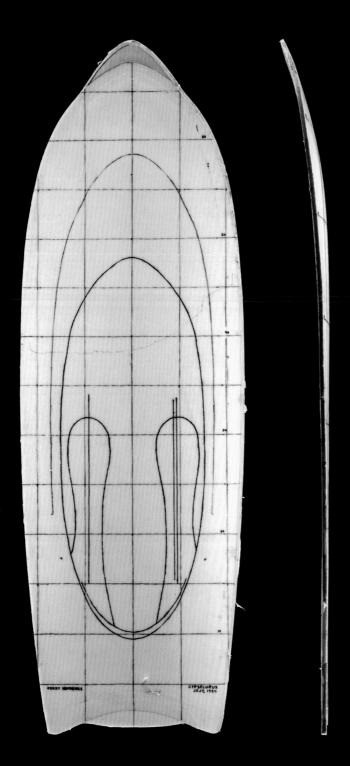

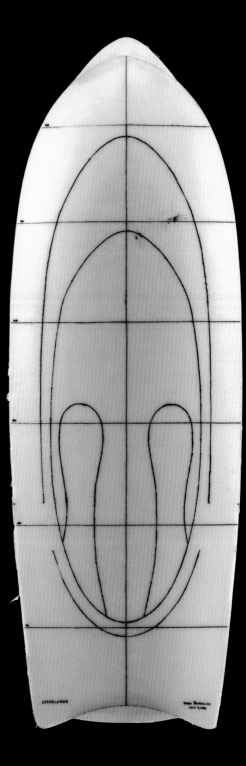

TERRY HENDRICKS

Bodyboard

1980s; 48"; Polyurethane foam, resin, fiberglass

COLLECTION OF TY PONDER

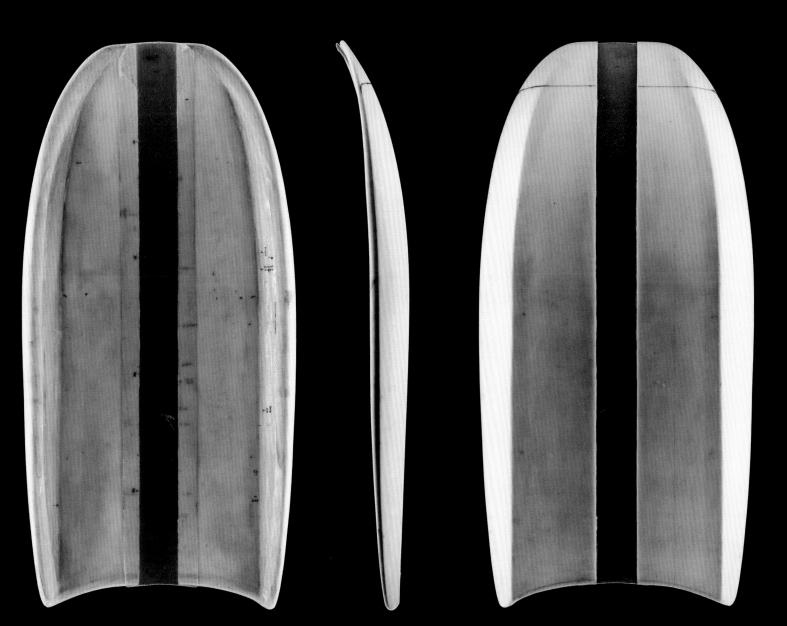

"Pelicanfoil" bodyboard with hydrofoils fore and aft

2000s; 48"; Polyurethane foam, resin, fiberglass, aluminum

COLLECTION OF TY PONDER

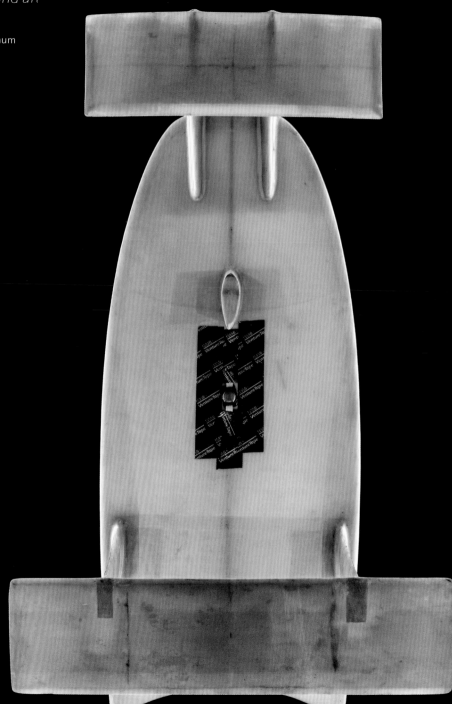

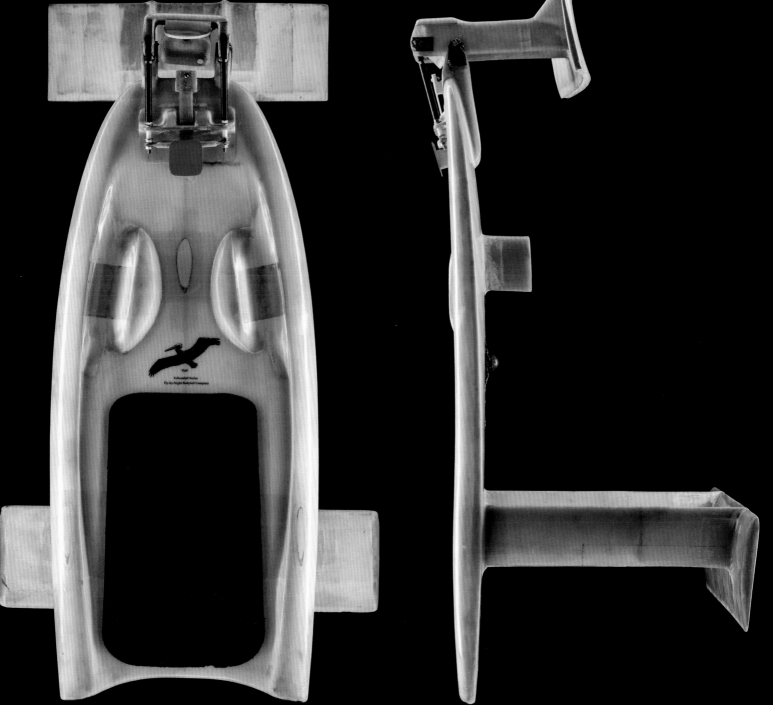

Fish

1970s; 64"; Polyurethane foam, resin, fiberglass, marine plywood

COLLECTION OF ERIC "BIRD" HUFFMAN

Plates 41–44
Boards by Steve Lis, 1969–2006

114|

Steve Lis is the patriarch of a uniquely local family of surfboards born in south San Diego County. He is the point of origin and creative force behind the fish, the first truly functional multifinned surfboard of the shortboard era. In basic principle, the fish was an effective design right from the start. Today, a talented surfer like Dave Rastovich or Ryan Burch can jump on a forty-year-old Lis fish and flow through an entire repertoire of twenty-first-century moves, though noticeably smoother and slightly more horizontal than on a stock shortboard. As demonstrated by "Rasta" and Burch, the fish style of surfing is aesthetically very pleasing to the eye, now more than ever.

Well into his fifth decade of refining and evolving his design, Lis remains true to the distinct craft and design ethic he started with in 1967. He keeps a shaping room in Hawai'i, where he lives, and in San Diego, where he returns a few times a year. He shapes custom boards for his friends and a short list of lucky surfers who seek him out.

Lis never followed the mainstream—never used a close tolerance blank from Clark Foam to shape a toothpick shortboard—never copied an MR twin, an Aipa sting, or a Simon Anderson thruster—never copied anyone, in fact. And yet, some of the most memorable and influential surfing of the shortboard era has resulted from his designs. His own surfing is legendary, though thinly documented, by choice. Lis avoided cameras. Or, to put it another way, cameras were not allowed at the places he liked to surf. They still are not, both in San Diego and Hawai'i. There are surfers riding amazing waves in the islands, now, on Lis boards, at places where cameras are simply not tolerated.

Other fish riders were caught on film, however. Mike Tabeling, David Nuuhiwa, and Jimmy Blears rode fish and surfed circles around single fins in the early 1970s. "Bunker" Spreckels redefined point-break surfing on a 5'6" Lis fish at Jeffreys Bay in South Africa in 1975. Just under two decades later, Tom Curren and Derek Hynd were filmed surfing Jeffreys on fishes, performances that left the thruster generation of the early 1990s scratching their heads in amazement.

And so, even in 2014, the fish mystique is alive and well. It lives more by word of mouth and eyewitness accounts than by media coverage. Over the years, the design has been heavily commercialized, at times, by the surfboard industry. Lis shrugs it off. In his world, things are the same as always.

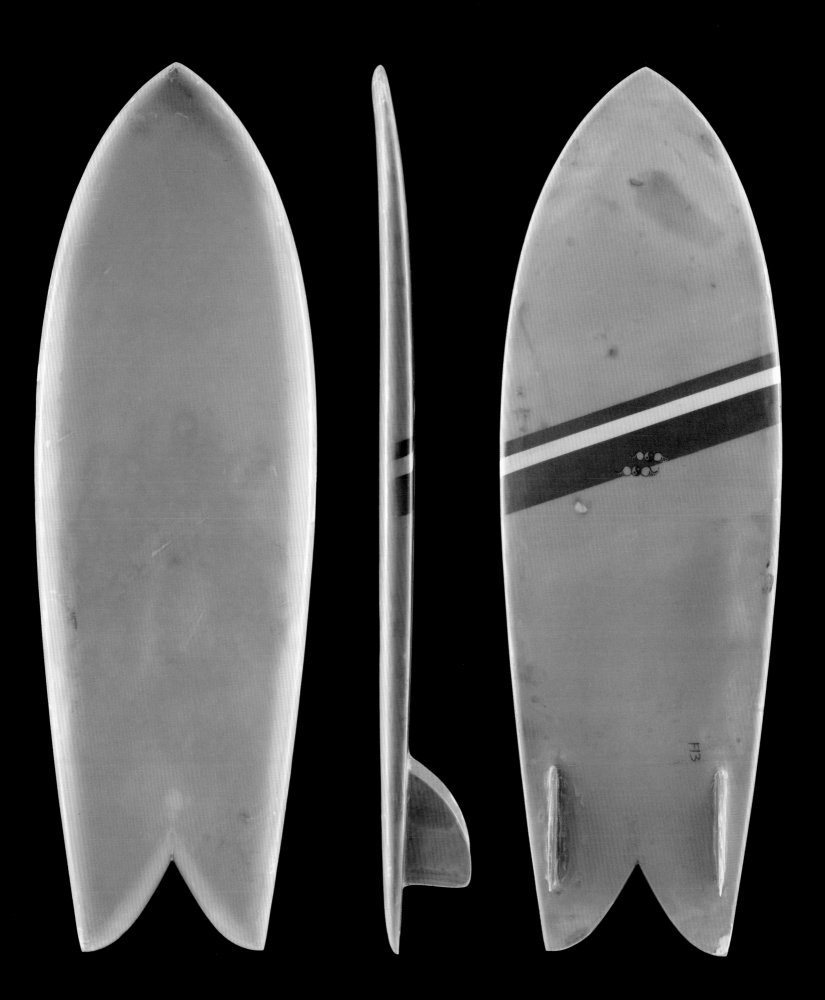

STEVE LIS

Gun fish

1970s; 75"; Polyurethane foam, resin, fiberglass

COLLECTION OF ERIC "BIRD" HUFFMAN

STEVE LIS SHAPE, LARRY GEPHART FINS AND SIDE BITES

Gun fish with side bites

2002; 81" × 21" × 2.75"; Polyurethane foam, resin, fiberglass

COLLECTION OF LARRY GEPHART

STEVE LIS SHAPE, LARRY GEPHART KEELS

Fish

2005; 66" × 22" × 2.5"; Polyurethane foam, resin, fiberglass, marine plywood

PRIVATE COLLECTION

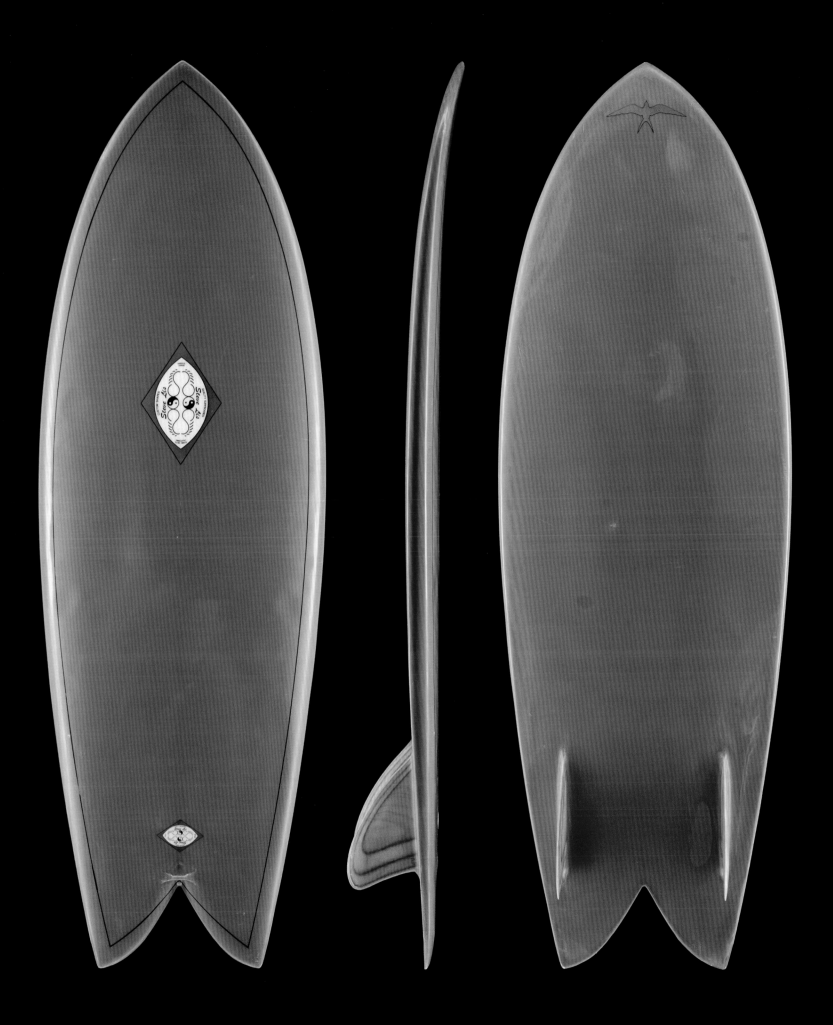

Plates 45–49
San Diego Fish Boards, 1969–2006

122| This school of fish shares a common ances-
tor. They are the indigenous offspring of fish
number one, born in San Diego County, the
native spawning ground of their species.
Beginning with Steve Lis and the first fish
in 1967, the design has been evolving in San
Diego for over forty-five years. Skip Frye,
Larry Gephart, and Cher and Steve Pendarvis were there at the beginning. They continue to ride and refine all sorts of variations
on the original design, including boards that
are adapted specifically for certain surf spots
and conditions. The fish in all its forms is so
well suited for the wide range of conditions
in San Diego County that some surfers have
never ridden anything else.

The boards shown here range from early
"back yard" kneeboards and stand-up boards
by Mike Thorton and Louis Greco, to "side
bite" collaborations between Steve Lis, Larry
Gephart, Skip Frye, and Stanley Pleskunas.
Collaboration and experimentation is a long-
standing tradition among the original fish
riders in San Diego.

MIKE THORTON

Fish

1969; 68" × 20" × 2.75"; Polyurethane foam, resin,
fiberglass, color tint

COLLECTION OF ERIC "BIRD" HUFFMAN

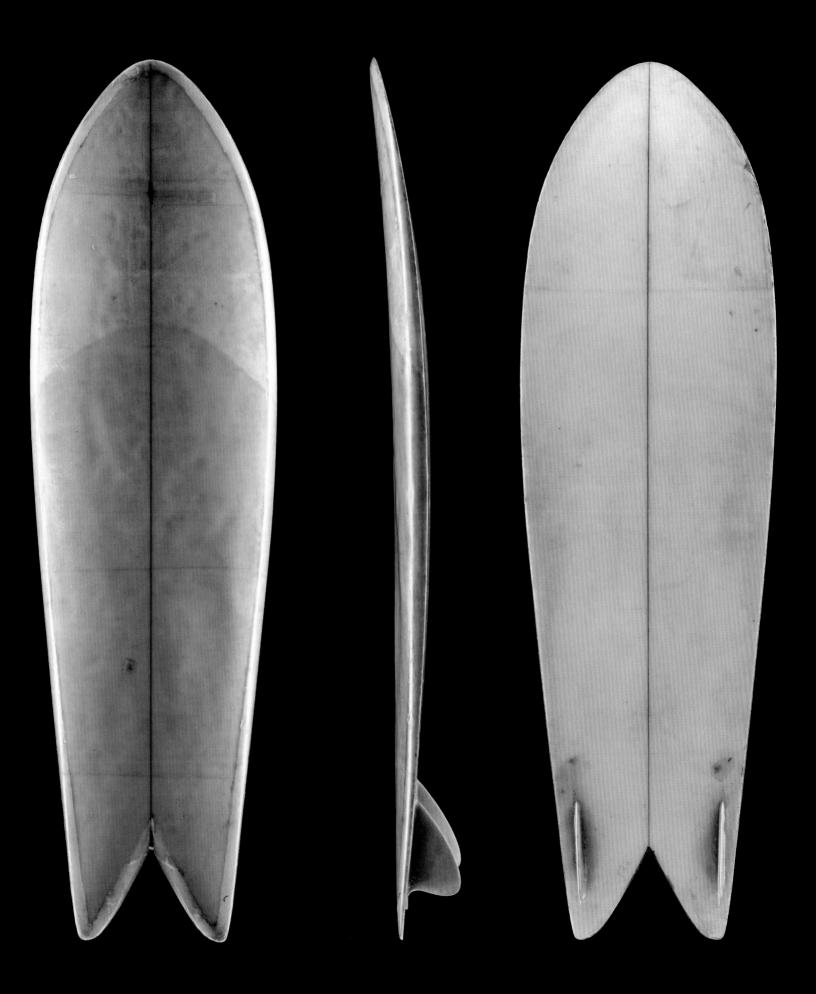

LOUIS GRECO

Fish

1970; 56" × 20" × 2.75"; Polyurethane foam, resin, fiberglass

COLLECTION OF HANS NEWMAN

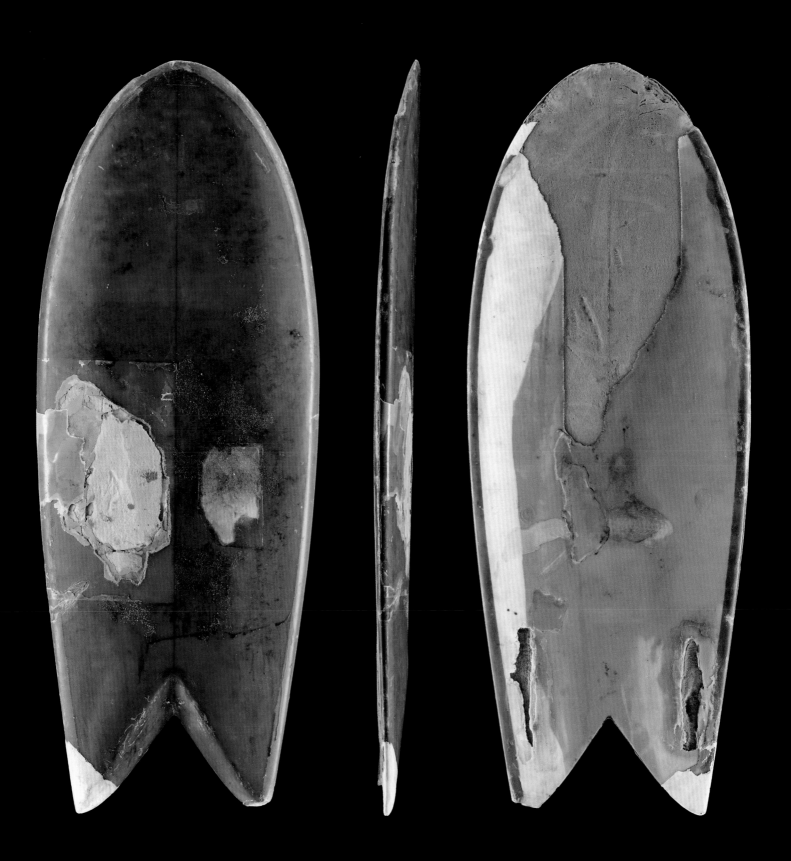

LARRY GEPHART

Fish

1970s; 64" × 21" × 2.5"; Polyurethane foam, resin, fiberglass

COLLECTION OF LARRY GEPHART

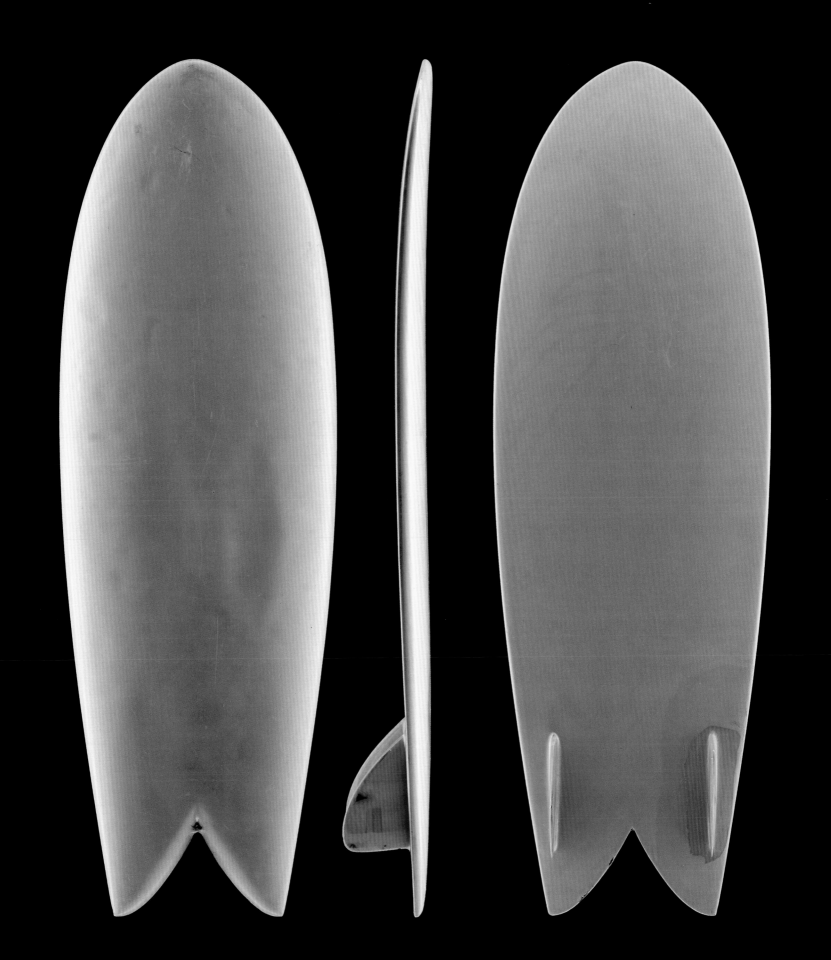

SKIP FRYE SHAPE, LARRY GEPHART SIDE BITES

Gun fish with side bites

1990s; 81" × 20.5" × 2.5"; Polyurethane foam, resin, fiberglass

COLLECTION OF LARRY GEPHART

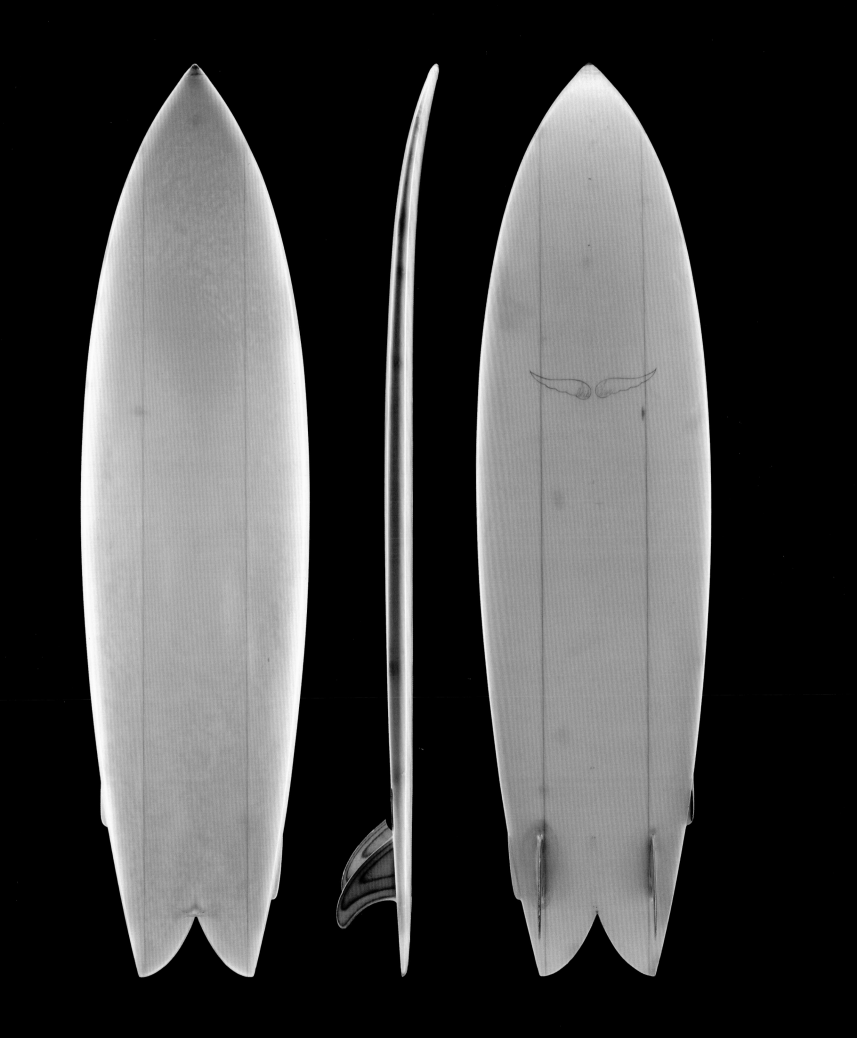

SKIP FRYE SHAPE, STANLEY PLESKUNAS FINS, LARRY GEPHART SIDE BITES

Longfish

2004; 81" × 21.25" × 2.5"; Polyurethane foam, resin, fiberglass, PVC foam, PVC

COLLECTION OF SKIP FRYE

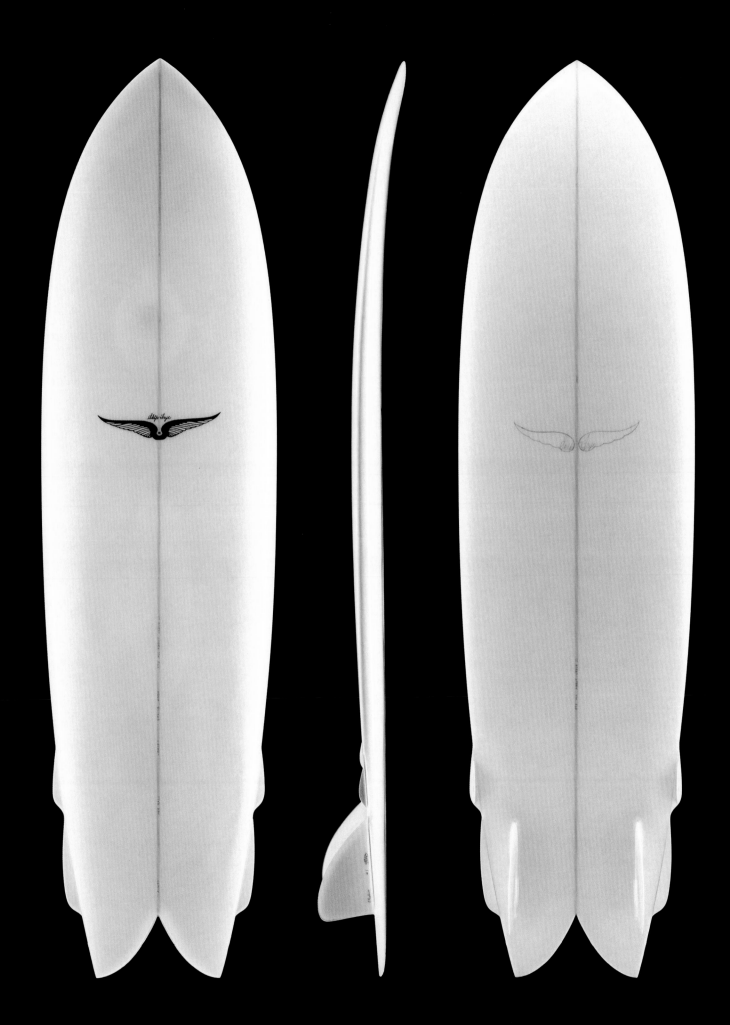

Plates 50–54
The Tools of a Profession: Stinging,
Swooping, Zapping, and Thrusting
in the IPS Arena, 1976–1982

132|

"Yeah, I tried going onto twinfins—a desperate measure, I was a desperate man (laughs). The main problem with that was jumping from one board to the other. I thought I could do it but I couldn't. The problem was that after you surf the twinfin your single would feel like it had an anchor on the back."

—Simon Anderson, interview with Surfing World Magazine, *Australia*

Professional surfing as we know it began in 1976, when Australian Peter Townend was crowned the first world surfing champion by the International Professional Surfers (IPS). A series of international tournaments had been strung together that year, with points awarded for results. Townend came out on top. The IPS (1976–82) was the original world governing body of professional surfing. During its reign, the modern finned surfboard would be transformed, in the context of competitive surfing, by the small-wave performance needs of early professional surfers. With livelihoods at stake, and big-purse events outside Hawai'i often held at urban beaches, the early pros were forced to reevaluate their equipment and question the rule of thumb. A sleek single fin was fine for Sunset, Haleiwa, and Pipeline on Oahu's North Shore, but it was useless for blown-out Narrabeen or two-foot Burleigh on Australia's east coast. That being said, the small-wave innovations born in the IPS would rapidly cross over into big-wave designs.

Hawaiians Reno Abellira, Ben Aipa, and Larry Bertlemann were among the first to initiate design changes that would impact the competitive arena of the IPS. These changes would come not from big-wave designs bred in the Country (Oahu's North Shore) but from small-wave designs bred in Town (Oahu's South Shore). Town is a fitting venue, given its history as a surfing ground. It was here that short *alaia* and *paha* boards skimmed across gentle, perfectly groomed wave faces hundreds of years ago; here that Lindsay Lord conducted his planing plate tests in 1945; here that Valentine Ching and Wally Froiseth honed their stand-up *paipo* skills in the 1950s; here that Abellira and Bertlemann bore witness to those skills and rode *paipo* boards themselves; and here that Aipa pondered the hydrodynamics of powerboat hulls he saw in Kewalo Basin and Pearl Harbor in the 1960s and 1970s.

By 1975, Aipa's interest in powered planing hulls had led him to create the sting, a single-fin swallowtail with a pronounced planing surface set forward from a conspicuous pair of "wings" placed about a third of the way up the board. The sting was really two boards in one: a wide *paha/paipo*–like planing surface in front, and a much narrower board in back. It was "Town" in the front, "Country" in the back. In Hawaiian, *paha* means "half-board." The front half of the sting reflects the flat, wide planing surface of the traditional *paha* design. The very noticeable forward planing area of the sting also marks another appearance of the universal *paipo/paha* planing shape that was defined in Western scientific terms by Lindsay Lord in *Naval Architecture of Planing Hulls* (1946). In a whirl of synchronicity (geographically centered on Oahu's South Shore) *paha*-like shapes were studied by Lord in the context of powered boat hulls. New boats were then designed, these boats inspired Aipa, and the *paha/paipo* shape reappeared in the sting as a speed-generating planing surface.

Bertlemann was the premier test pilot for the sting, and his loose, flowing, radical approach on the design is an iconic statement of progressive Hawaiian surfing. Extremely well documented and publicized, Bertlemann appeared on the cover of *Surfer* magazine, riding a sting, in 1975. In 1976 his protégés, "Buttons" Kaluhiokalani and Mark Liddell, also appeared on *Surfer*'s cover, sitting on the rocks near Ala Moana, both armed with stings. By that time, Aipa, Bertlemann, and the sting were synonymous with a new surf-skate style emerging from Town.

The Town design influence of Aipa was immediately put to use by Australian pro Mark Richards, who rode a series of Aipa designs in competition during the early years of the IPS. Meanwhile, Reno Abellira used his Town-bred *paipo* savvy to create a very short, wide, dual fin that he rode in IPS events in Australia in 1976. The designs of Aipa and Abellira, born of the high-performance surf

scene of Oahu's South Shore, made a solid connection in the mind of Richards. The sting had already pushed his small-wave surfing in radical new directions, and seeing Abellira's little twin fin inspired him to go even further. In the winter of 1976–77, Richards took shaping lessons from Dick Brewer in Hawai'i. Out of these sessions, the prototype for the most important transitional board in pro surfing history emerged: the MR twin.

Richards and his twin fin proceeded to dominate the remaining years of the IPS, winning the world title four years in a row, from 1979 through 1982. Brewer shaped the first version; Richards shaped the rest. Though somewhat similar boards had been made before by other shapers, Richards's refinement of the design and his deadly use of it as a competitive weapon was unprecedented. Suddenly the single-fin-dominated IPS was infiltrated by a small-wave design that rendered the status quo obsolete almost overnight. The MR twin accomplished a number of things historically. Though the details differ somewhat, the MR twin brought Simmons's outboard fin, rail-to-rail concepts into the mainstream, where they remain to this day. After Richards, nobody won a world title on a single fin again.

Richards had a very unique surfing style, and his twin-fin design suited him perfectly. But the MR twin wasn't for everyone. Other pros, most notably young Australian phenomenon Cheyne Horan, refused to abandon the solid, central pivot point of the single fin. Horan and his shaper, Geoff McCoy, had developed an extremely futuristic single fin that came to be known as the "Laser Zap." In its later incarnation, the Laser Zap used an innovative winged-keel fin to control an extremely wide tail. Planing surface and width were all pushed back toward the tail. About halfway up the board, the outline abruptly narrowed to a very pointed nose. The Laser Zap was the opposite of the sting: it was Country in the front, Town in the back. Horan surfed it from the tail, and with the nose seemingly irrelevant, it also became known as a "no nose."

The Laser Zap worked, and Horan's surfing on it was arguably the most explosive and progressive ever done on a single fin, especially in the realm of professional surfing. Once again, a wide, rectangular planing surface, à la Lindsay Lord, was a key ingredient. Between them, the MR twin and the

Laser Zap cleanly demonstrated that width and planing in the fin area was essential for competitive shortboards in the IPS. But if the MR twin was not for every pro, at least it gained a large following among the competitors. The Laser Zap, for the most part, remained a novel experiment used only by Horan.

Another early pro that was reluctant to give up the single fin was Simon Anderson, a quintessential power surfer, board designer, and craftsman from Narrabeen, Australia. Anderson took the raging twin-fin wildfire ignited by MR and contained it in a controlled burn: the thruster. A very simplified version of how he created the design is as follows: He looked to the single-fin designs of McCoy and Horan and pulled the wide point back toward the tail. He used two forward fins like the MR, but added a third fin in the center, set back on a wide, blunt tail, for a total of three fins. He then reduced and equalized the size of all the fins. Voila—performance went through the roof. In 1981 at the Rip Curl Pro at Bells Beach

in Victoria, in huge, perfect surf, Anderson showed the world exactly what the future of pro surfing looked like. In the big picture, the thruster, the surfboard of the future, would ride on obscure innovations explored in the past. The planing surface of the traditional Hawaiian boards, the rail-to-rail principles of Simmons, and the rockers, curves, and controlled pivot point of the single fin all worked together in the thruster. The thruster satisfied just about everyone.

By 1983 the IPS was no more, and the current governing body, the ASP (Association of Surfing Professionals) took over. Thousands of boards and millions of dollars later, the thruster remains the standard design for professional surfers.

MARK RICHARDS

MR twin fin

late 1970s; 73" × 20" × 2.75"; Polyurethane foam, resin, fiberglass

SURFING HERITAGE & CULTURE CENTER

MIKE DIFFENDERFER

Twin fin

1979; 62" × 20" × 2.75"; Polyurethane foam, resin, fiberglass

COLLECTION OF HANK WARNER

GEOFF MCCOY

Laser Zap single fin

early 1980s; 66" × 20.5" × 2.60"; Polyurethane foam, resin, fiberglass

SURFING HERITAGE & CULTURE CENTER

140 |

SIMON ANDERSON

Thruster tri fin

1981; 71" × 19.5" × 2.75"; Polyurethane foam, resin, fiberglass

SURFING HERITAGE & CULTURE CENTER

see him alive. Without Elwell's lifelong dedication to documenting, understanding, and sharing Simmons's design legacy, surfing would be missing out on a crucial facet of its evolutionary design heritage.

Elwell had two Simmons boards in the early 1950s. One was a modified redwood plank that was over ten feet long. The second board was a custom nine-foot board, built in 1950 especially for Elwell and his girlfriend, Margie Manoch. This board was a light, refined planing hull made of balsa. Eventually, the board ended up in Hawai'i, where it lay under a house for many years and suffered termite damage. Elwell went to Hawai'i, retrieved it, and brought it back to California. In 2001, master craftsman and shaper Joe Bauguess restored it. All of the boards shown were then surfed, and for the first time since the mid-1950s, surfers experienced pure Simmons design. Simmons's interest in short planing hulls was also explored. (The only surviving example is the eight-foot Meistrell board shown on page 74.) Inspired by the Meistrell board, and by stories of even shorter boards, including a 5'6" balsa dual fin made by Al Nelson in 1957—Nelson knew Simmons and was familiar with his dual-finned concepts—a series of short "mini-Simmons" boards was made from 2006 to 2010.

In 2009 Ryan Burch used special closed-cell foam to make surfable replicas of Lindsay Lord's A5 planing plate from 1946, one of the basic cornerstones of Simmons's planing metric designs and Daniel Thomson's modern planing hulls are two examples. Thomson was among the first surfers to ride the replicas commissioned by Elwell. By scaling Simmons's boards down within the constraints of their existing aspect ratios, Thomson is creating a new blueprint for the shortboard. Alternately, surfers around the world began making Simmons-inspired boards at home in their garages. The functional simplicity of Simmons's design was demystifying the cult of shaping.

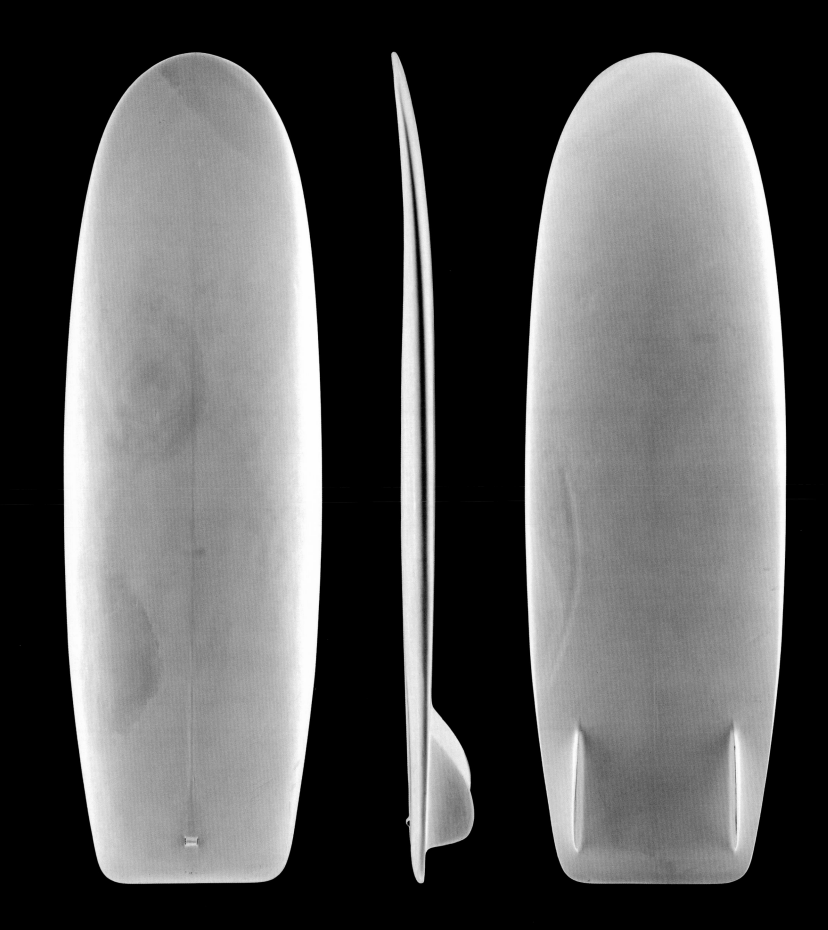

JOE BAUGUESS

"Mini" hydrodynamic planing hull

2007; 63" × 23.5" × 3"; EPS foam, fiberglass, epoxy resin

HYDRODYNAMICA PROJECT

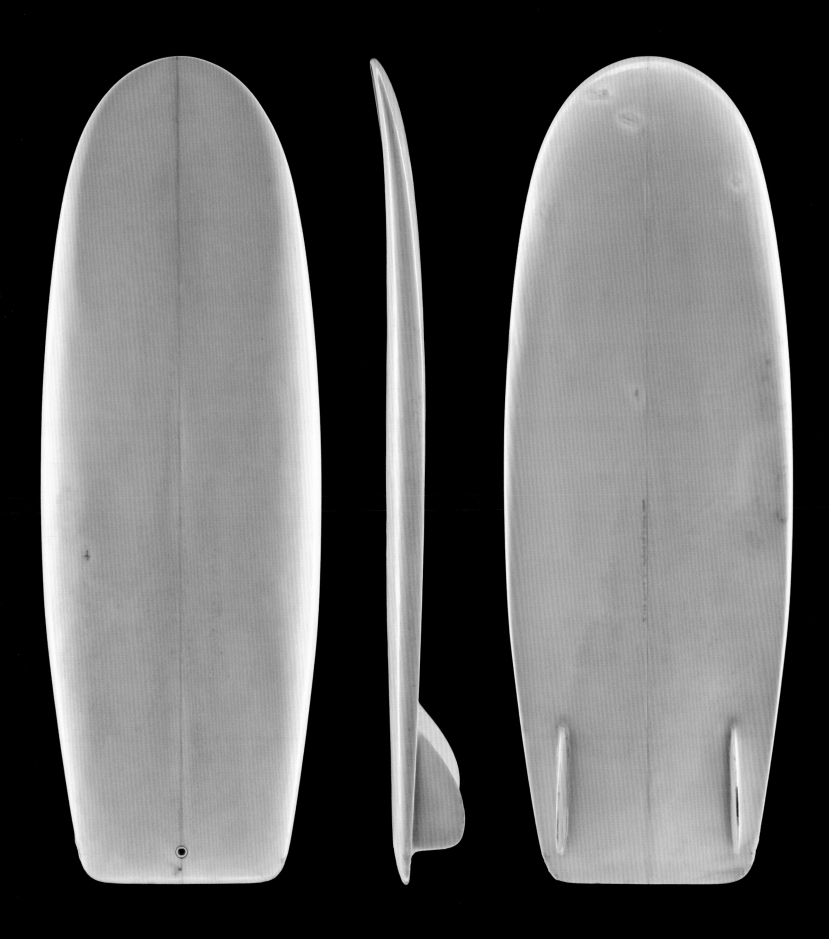

LARRY MABILE SHAPE, LARRY GEPHART KEELS

White Pony fish/planing hull hybrid

2007; 59" × 23.5" × 3"; EPS foam, epoxy resin, fiberglass

HYDRODYNAMICA PROJECT

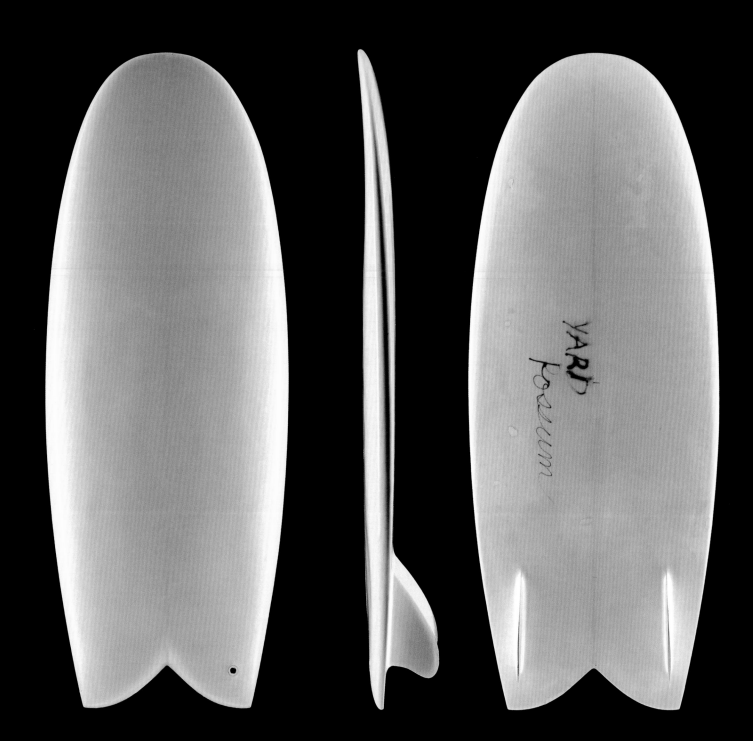

Modern planing hull

2007; 66" × 18" × 2.5"; Polyurethane foam, resin, fiberglass

HYDRODYNAMICA PROJECT

RYAN BURCH

Lindsay Lord planing plate

2009; 52" × 22" × 2"; Black closed-cell foam

HYDRODYNAMICA PROJECT

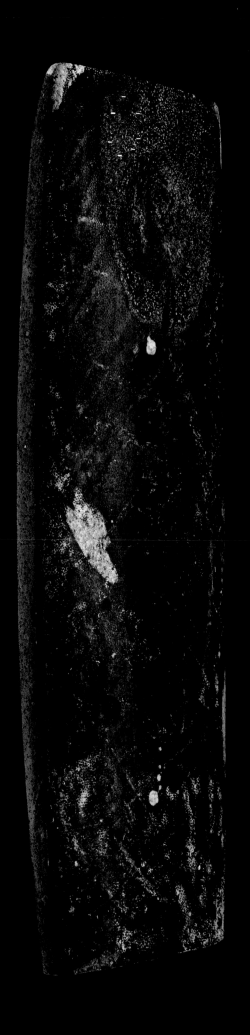

LUCAS DIRKSE

Lindsay Lord planing plate

2009; 48" × 22" × 2.5"; INT foam

HYDRODYNAMICA PROJECT

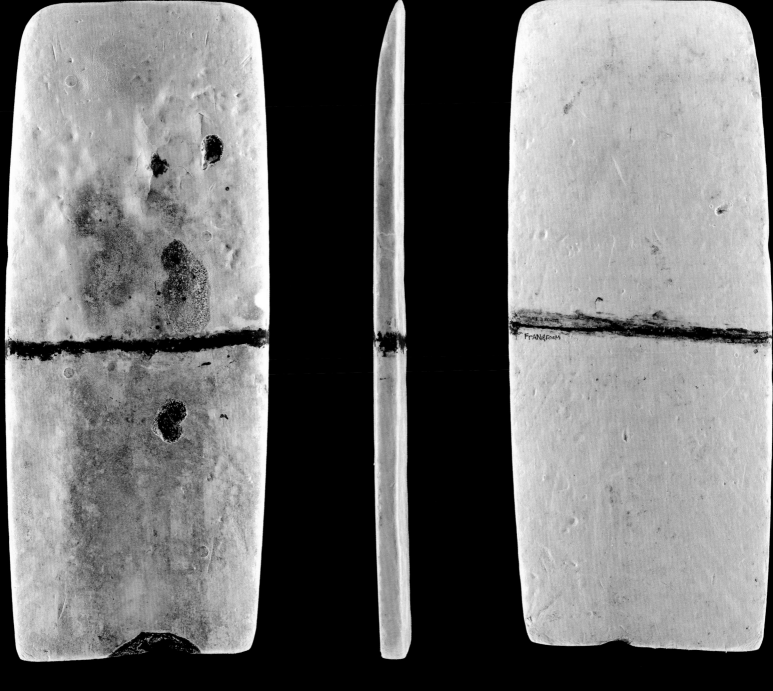

FrAN&FoaM

Plates 62–63
Boards by Mike Griffin, 2009–2011

152| Mike Griffin is a soft-spoken kneeboarder who has quietly and respectfully followed the design path and ethics of his San Diego mentors. Griffin is a low-key purist, following the tradition of fish shaping and riding that began with Steve Lis, "Bunker" Spreckels, Skip Frye, Larry Gephart, and others in the 1960s. He is a living example of Sōetsu Yanagi's craft ideals, as articulated in *The Unknown Craftsman*. His beautifully crafted, unsigned boards are worthy, functional tributes to those who came before him.

MIKE GRIFFIN

Fish

2011; 57" × 21" × 2.50"; Polyurethane foam, resin, fiberglass

COLLECTION OF MIKE GRIFFIN

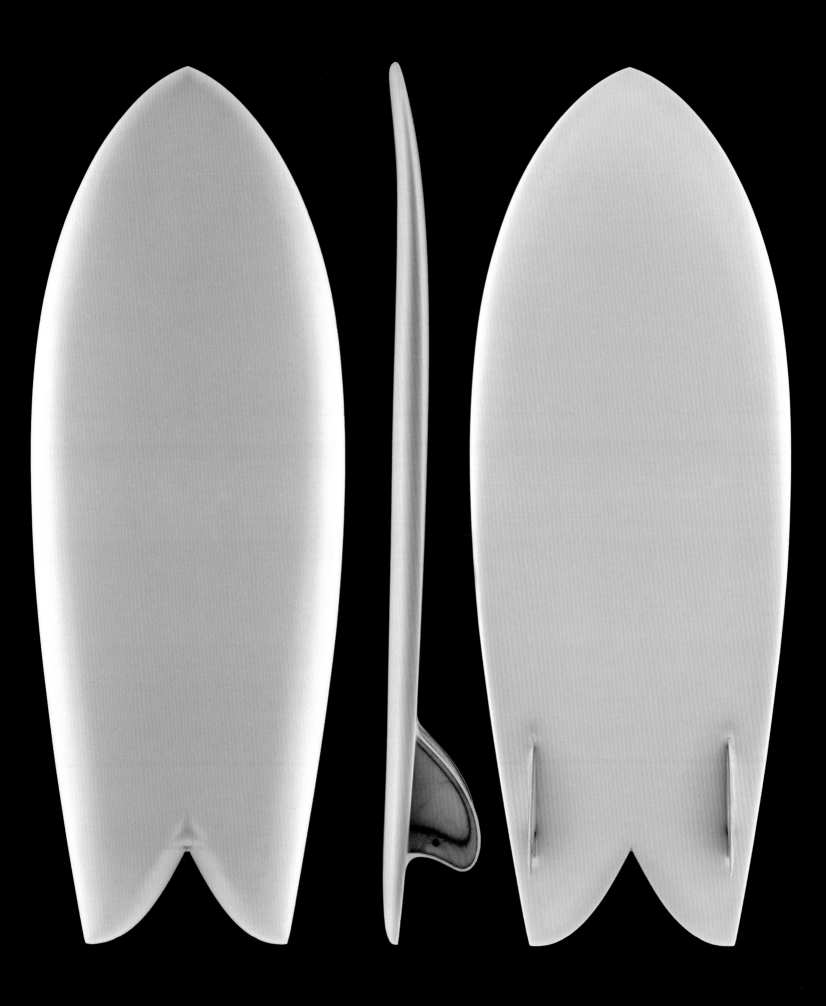

MIKE GRIFFIN

Hydrodynamic planing hull

2009; 73" × 23" × 3"; Polyurethane foam, resin, fiberglass

COLLECTION OF MIKE GRIFFIN

156|

Carl Ekstrom, age seventy-one, and his protégé Ryan Burch, age twenty-three, are exploring an infinite number of complementary curves, rockers, and fin combinations in their asymmetric surfboards. Ekstrom, who has been working on surfboards since 1952, began dabbling in asymmetry in 1965. By 1966, he had received an U.S. patent for the concept (it is very unusual for a patent to be awarded for a surfboard design feature). The idea behind asymmetry in surfboards starts with the human body. When surfing, the "toe side" and "heel side" use very different parts of the anatomy, with different centers of gravity. Modern surfing is rail to rail, constantly shifting weight from the toes to the heels, and vice versa. Asymmetry attempts to optimize each side of the board according to the very different weight distribution and anatomical tools on the front and back sides of the body. Heels and toes are very different; hence, the heel side and toe side of an asymmetric surfboard will be different, too.

In 2007 Ekstrom began experimenting with asymmetric versions of the fish and the Simmons planing hull. In 2009 he started sharing his knowledge with Burch, who was also experimenting with fish and Simmons-inspired boards. An unusually gifted surfer and a natural craftsman, Burch immediately demonstrated the validity of the asymmetric concept through his surfing performances. Ekstrom and Burch share a start-to-finish handcrafted ethic, often building boards from scratch, making their own fins, and glassing and sanding their boards. Ekstrom also crafts quarter-scale models of all his designs.

In the realm of handcrafted surfboard construction technique, Ekstrom is a master. He is a living encyclopedia of processes and materials. His glassing skills are unsurpassed. That being said, he is hardly a throwback to another era. His design mentality continues to evolve in a highly progressive and creative way, and he is constantly seeking out and using the latest high-tech materials. Ekstrom has inspired a much younger generation to taste the fruits of asymmetry. For big-wave surfer Ben Wilkinson, finless aficionado Derek Hynd, and young aerialist Lucas Dirkse, asymmetric designs have opened up new possibilities.

Burch is taking asymmetric design even further. Recently, he designed, shaped, glassed, and sanded (in less than four months) more than forty personal experimental asymmetric boards. No two are alike, and they cover the entire design spectrum, from big-wave guns to small-wave performers. Such an explosive creative outburst of board building and design has probably never been equaled in surfing. He is currently riding them in western Australia and Indonesia. Recent reports from Bali tell of Burch, on the largest swell of the season, connecting waves from the Bombie through Outside Corner at Uluwatu on a 6'2" asymmetric dual fin. Those familiar with the break under such conditions will know this to be an unprecedented milestone.

In 1968, Andy Warhol went to La Jolla and purchased two boards from Ekstrom to use as props for his film *San Diego Surf*. Warhol then asked Ekstrom to build more boards to exhibit as art in a New York gallery, in the context of minimalist Pop sculpture. Given the rise of California minimalism at the time, with the surfboard-inspired polyester resin and fiberglass sculpture of "finish fetish" artists like John McCracken, it made sense that Warhol appreciated Ekstrom's work. But the show was not to be. Valerie Solanas shot Warhol just days after he returned from La Jolla to New York. The attack almost killed him, and his plans for exhibiting Ekstrom's boards in New York fell by the wayside.

But what if the show *had* happened? Would gorgeous, oversized, "minimalist-Pop-surfboard-inspired-sculptures" by Ekstrom hang on museum walls around the world and grace the pages of coffee-table art books? Would college art professors give long-winded lectures about them? Would they be traded as commodities, with ever-increasing monetary value attached to them as Ekstrom received critical accolades and soaked up recognition as an "important finish fetish artist"? Would his "work" be analyzed and contextualized by critics and bought and sold by dealers, galleries, and museums?

The Ekstrom show that never happened brings up some interesting questions. What is it that makes a plank by McCracken thirty times more valuable than a planing hull by Bob Simmons or a fiberglass spoon by George Greenough? One is within the institutionalized value system, the other is not. Like money itself, the value is based entirely on an intangible concept. One object is art; the other is just a surfboard. One man is an artist; the other is just a surfer. One endeavor is an elaborate exercise in individual creative expression and conceptual gymnastics; the other is just a pastime.

And yet, the objects created by surfers like Ekstrom blur the line between fine art and "mere" functional design. Their value transcends money and institutional value systems. They had little effect on the abstract "concept" of surfing, but a great deal of effect on the act itself. Ironically, if handcrafted surfboards can be perceived through the *mingei* philosophy set forth by Sōetsu Yanagi in *The Unknown Craftsman*, then perhaps mass-produced industrial crafts are best perceived through Warhol's Pop philosophy. As Warhol put it, "Pop Art is for everyone."

Ekstrom has spent his life making things with his hands, always with the intent that those things be used for a purpose, and always with the desire that they last longer and perform better than what he may have made before. Beauty is a natural byproduct of his processes. Beautiful objects are even more so when they are useful, and perhaps they are of more value to human beings than art for art's sake, and certainly of more value than art for money's sake. Ekstrom chuckles when he recalls a contemporary art museum director telling him years ago that "art is anything that's really useless." Ekstrom's perspective is that of the designer and the craftsman. So what if his New York "art" show never happened? Sixty years after mixing his first batch of resin, Ekstrom will be back in his workshop at first light, building surfboards with his hands that rival or surpass the work of any "finish fetish" fine artist. And for the pastime's sake, they will hit the lip and get barreled, too. Surfers can appreciate that.

CARL EKSTROM

Asymmetric longboard

1965; 111" × 21" × 3"; Polyurethane foam, resin, fiberglass

COLLECTION OF MICHAEL BONAGUIDI

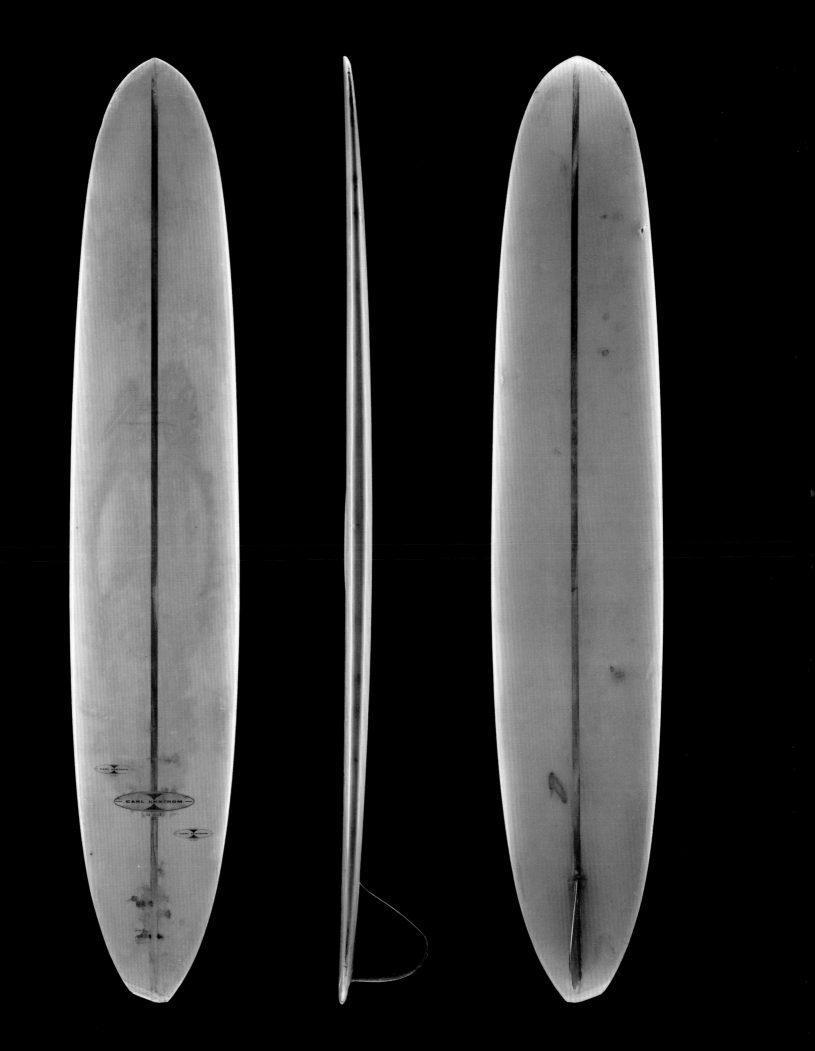

CARL EKSTROM

Asymmetric "s" tail quad fin

2013; 85" × 20.25" × 2.5"; Polyurethane foam, resin, fiberglass, bamboo fins

COLLECTION OF CARL EKSTROM

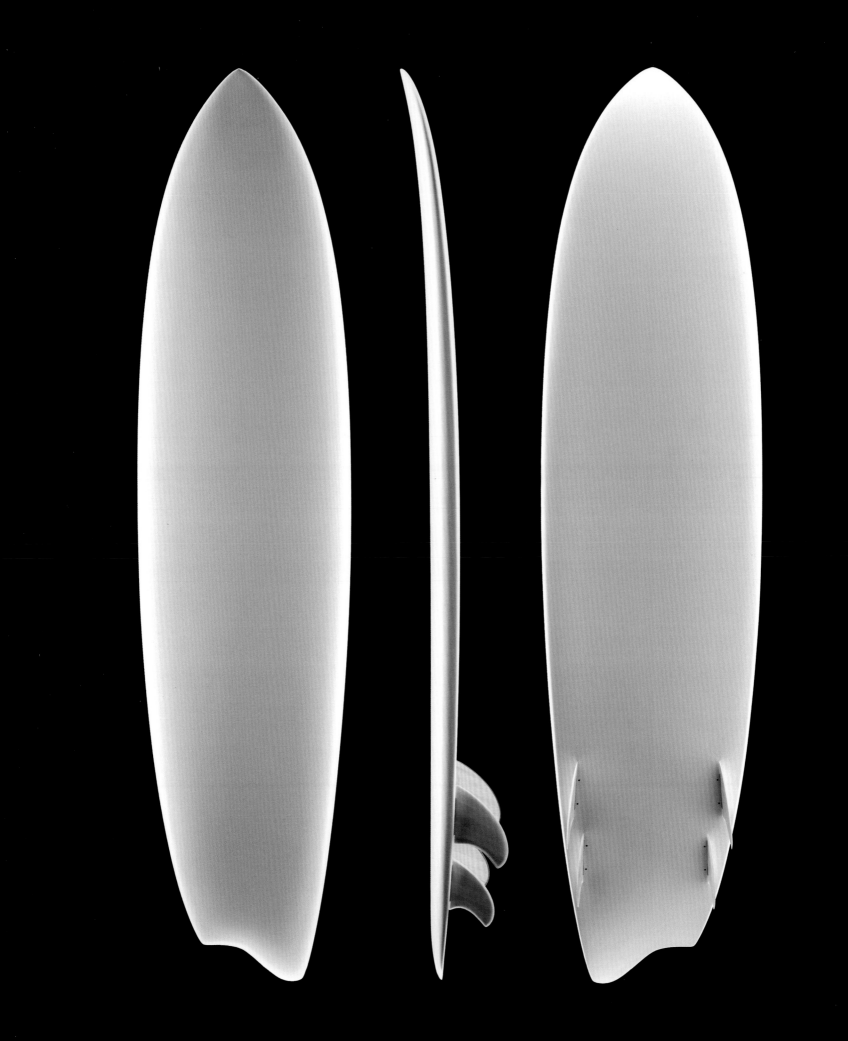

CARL EKSTROM, STANLEY PLESKUNAS, TAYLOR/DYKEMA

Asymmetric wakeboard

1990s; 56" × 15.75" × 1.1"; Wood laminate

COLLECTION OF CARL EKSTROM

ekström

PLESKUNAS

CARL EKSTROM

*Finless asymmetric board for machine-generated
standing waves*

1990s; 42" × 15.5" × 1.75"; Polypropylene foam

COLLECTION OF CARL EKSTROM

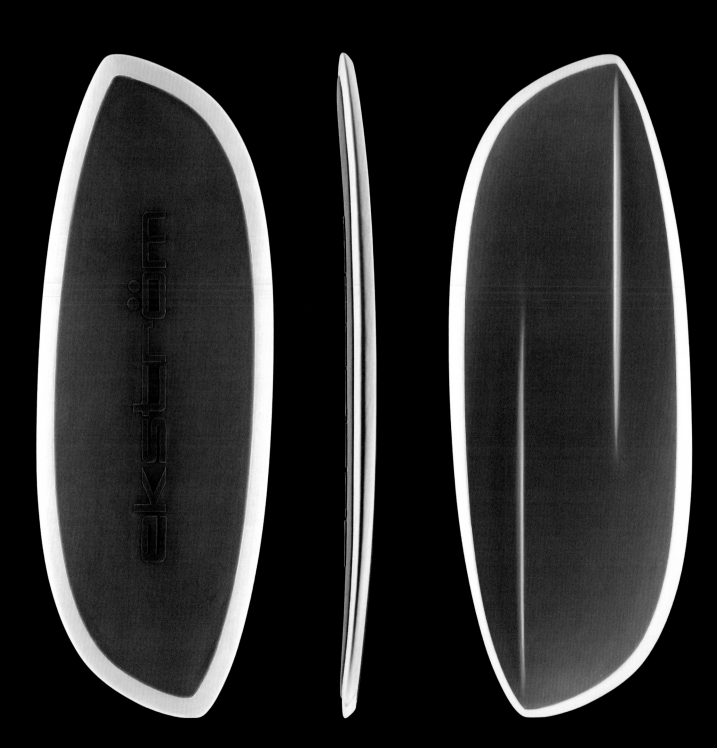

CARL EKSTROM

Asymmetric planing hull

2009; 68" × 20" × 2.5"; Polyurethane foam, resin, fiberglass, color tint

COLLECTION OF CARL EKSTROM

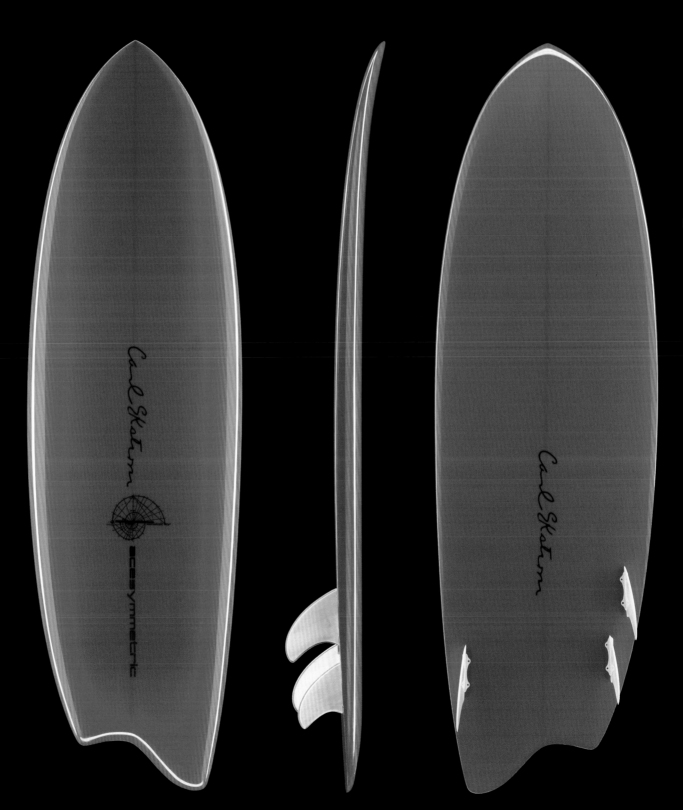

RYAN BURCH

Asymmetric fish

2008; 66" × 20" × 2.5"; Polyurethane foam, resin, fiberglass

COLLECTION OF RYAN BURCH

RYAN BURCH

"Sledge Hammer" asymmetric planing hull

2009; 59" × 20" × 2.5"; Polyurethane foam, resin, fiberglass

COLLECTION OF RYAN BURCH

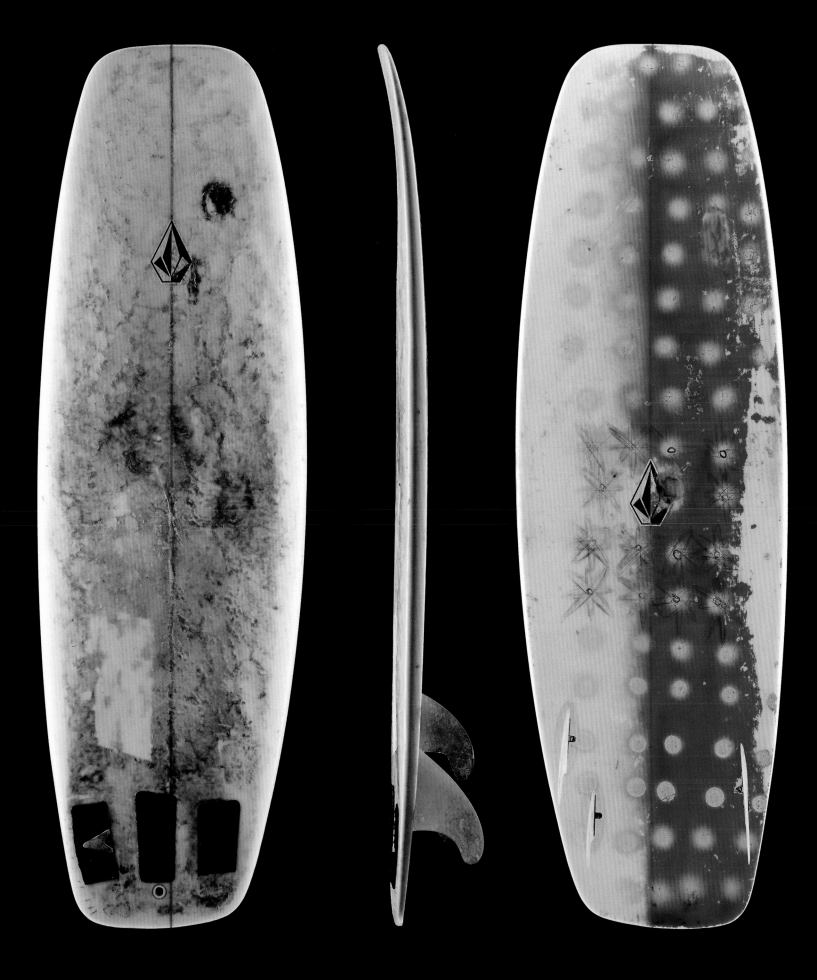

RYAN BURCH

Asymmetric planing hull

2010; 74" × 20" × 2.75"; Polyurethane foam, resin, fiberglass

PRIVATE COLLECTION

Asymmetric shortboard

2010; 65" × 18" × 2.5"; Polyurethane foam, carbon fiber, fiberglass, resin, color tint

COLLECTION OF RYAN BURCH

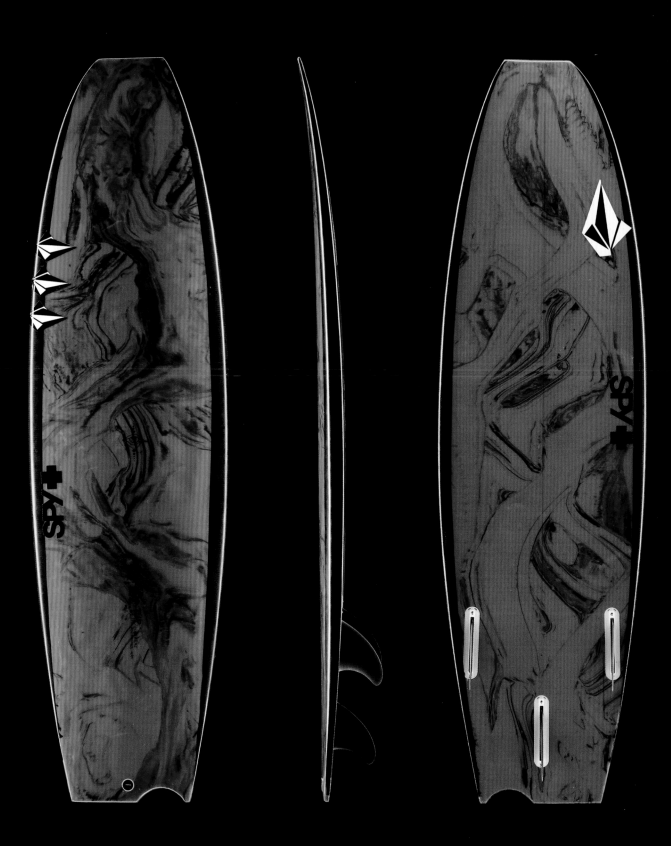

RYAN BURCH

Asymmetric shortboard

2011; 67" × 18.75" × 2.25"; Polyurethane foam, carbon fiber, fiberglass, resin

COLLECTION OF RYAN BURCH

RYAN BURCH

Asymmetric shortboard

2011; 65" × 18" × 2.5"; Polyurethane foam, resin, fiberglass

COLLECTION OF RYAN BURCH

RYAN BURCH

Asymmetric shortboard

2011; 66" × 17.75" × 2.25"; Polyurethane foam, resin, fiberglass

COLLECTION OF RYAN BURCH

|76| Over the past twenty years or so, finless wooden designs inspired by traditional Hawaiian boards have gradually appeared around the world. This revival is Hawaiian in origin. Tom "Pohaku" Stone (and others, including Wally Froiseth) began building true traditional *alaia* boards in Hawai'i. They looked to boards from the Pauahi Bishop Museum's collection as guides, followed ancient specifications, and used native woods and traditional construction methods. The building and riding of traditional *alaia* boards was reintroduced in Hawai'i, by Hawaiians. The rebirth of traditional boards in the islands was low key and intensely focused on native culture. In Stone's case, it was yet another manifestation of his ongoing anthropological research into traditional Hawaiian cultural practices.

But, just as surfing spread from the islands to the corners of the globe in the early twentieth century, so, too, would the boards of the Hawaiian renaissance in the twenty-first. In keeping with his role as an educator, Stone passed some of his knowledge on to veteran Australian craftsman Paul Joske, who had a deep interest in traditional wooden Hawaiian boards. Joske began building traditional-style boards from nontraditional paulownia wood; these were ridden by his very talented surfer sons, Sage and Heath. Paulownia wood has unique properties. It is light and buoyant, flexible, and relatively strong. It also resists water and warping. As such, it has helped propel an explosion of interest in the building and riding of finless wooden boards in recent years.

Tom Wegener, an American expatriate living in Queensland, also began building *alaia*-inspired boards from paulownia, and by 2007, his boards were spreading from Australia to America. Wegener's brother Jon was instrumental in spreading finless paulownia designs throughout California at the time. By 2009, segments in major surf film projects, including *Musica Surfica*, directed by Mick Sowry (2008), and *The Present*, directed by Thomas Campbell (2009), featured finless wooden boards made by the Joskes and Wegener. Seeing such boards in action sparked a wave of interest, and many surfers began experiencing, for the first time, the thrill of riding waves on thin wooden boards.

Rob Machado and Ryan Burch were among the first surfers in the San Diego area to ride such boards. The boards pictured here were made from 2007 to 2009 and ridden mostly in San Diego County. All of them are finless. The boards made by the Wegener brothers from paulownia wood feature side cuts similar to those on snowboards. Ekstrom's designs use vacuum track rails developed by his good friend Tom Morey, inventor of the boogie board.

RYAN BURCH

Finless board

2008; 63" × 18.5" × 1.5"; Polyurethane foam, resin,
fiberglass, printed cotton fabric

COLLECTION OF RYAN BURCH

JON WEGENER

Alaia-inspired finless board

2007; 80" × 18" × .75"; Paulownia

COLLECTION OF IAN MCCOLL

JON WEGENER

Alaia-inspired finless board

2009; 76" × 19" × .5"; Paulownia

PRIVATE COLLECTION

CARL EKSTROM

Finless board

2009; 68" × 18" × 1.5"; Polyurethane foam, resin, fiberglass, marine paint

COLLECTION OF CARL EKSTROM

CARL EKSTROM

Bodyboard

2010; 47" × 21" × 1.5"; Polyurethane foam, resin,
fiberglass, marine paint

COLLECTION OF CARL EKSTROM

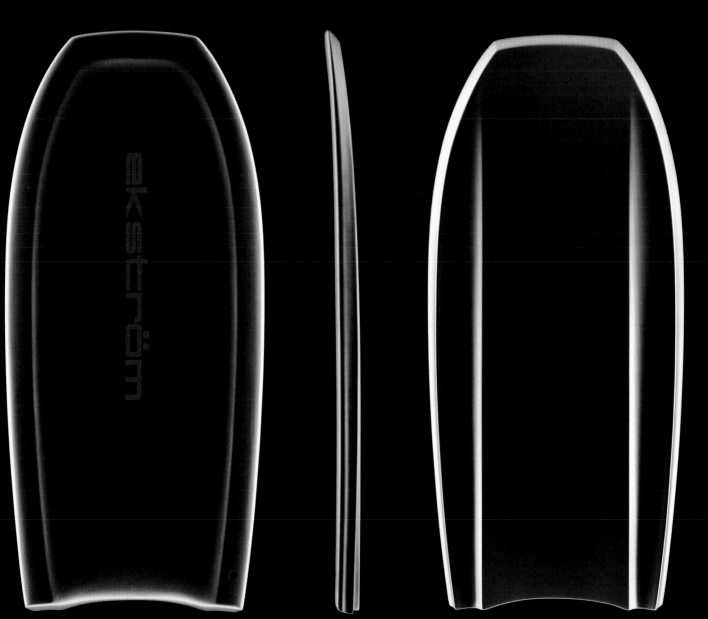

Australian Daniel Thomson, age thirty-one, is redefining the high-performance short-board. Picking up where Bob Simmons left off, Thomson minimizes the planing surface of his boards by maximizing their efficiency. He blends Simmons's concepts with proven post-Simmons design innovations, including Simon Anderson's tri-finned cluster and the wide, split tails inspired by the Steve Lis fish. Thomson studied Lindsay Lord's 1946 text on planing hulls, just as Simmons did before him. In simplest terms, Thomson's boards are what a conventional design looks like after the application of Simmons's theory.

DANIEL THOMSON

Modern planing hull with dual keels

2008; 67" × 19" × 2.75"; Polyurethane foam, resin, fiberglass, carbon fiber

PRIVATE COLLECTION

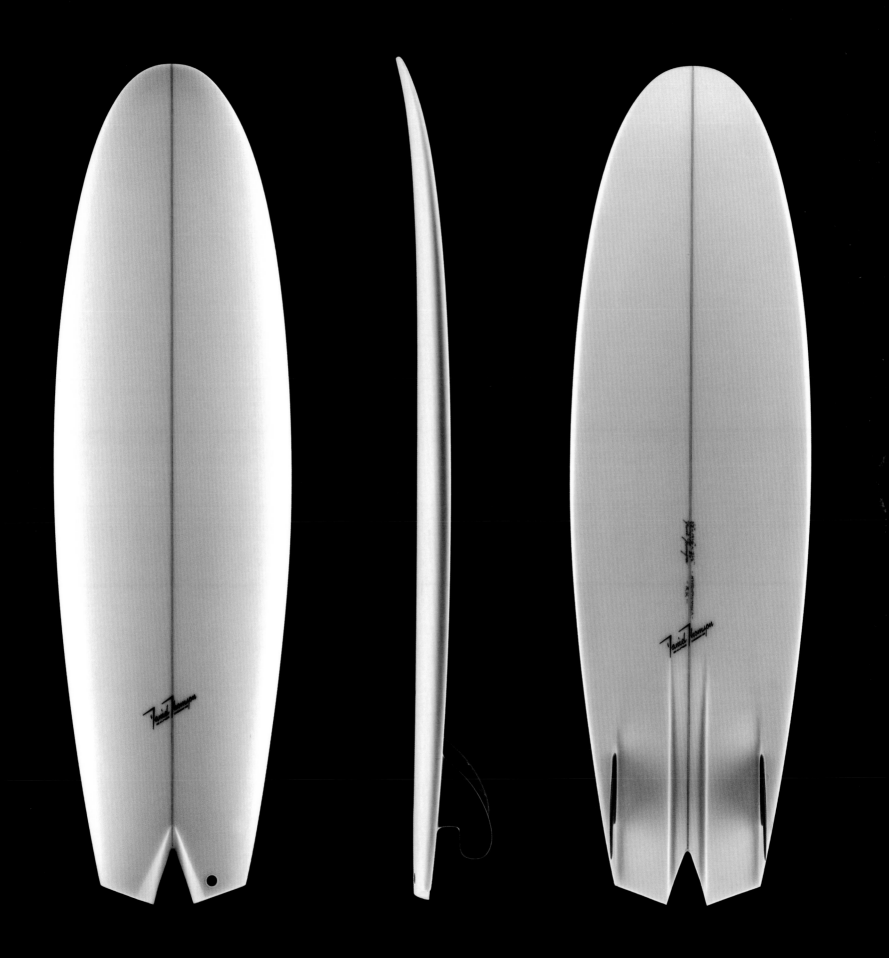

DANIEL THOMSON

Modern planing hull tri fin

2009; 62" × 17.5" × 2.25"; XTR foam, resin, fiberglass

COLLECTION OF DANIEL THOMSON

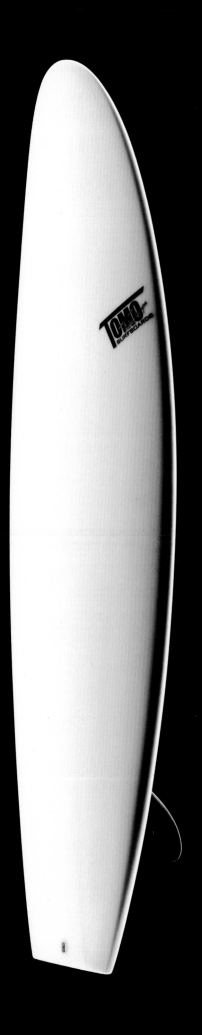

DANIEL THOMSON

"Fractal" modern planing hull

2011; 61" × 17.25" × 2"; XTR foam (unglassed)

COLLECTION OF DANIEL THOMSON

dern planing hull tri fin

2011; 68" × 19" × 2.75"; XTR foam, epoxy resin, fiberglass, bamboo

PRIVATE COLLECTION

DANIEL THOMSON

"Vader" modern planing hull

2009; 61" × 17.25" × 2.25"; XTR foam, resin, carbon fiber

COLLECTION OF DANIEL THOMSON

DANIEL THOMSON

"Vanguard" modern planing hull five fin

2011; 66" × 18.75" × 2.5"; XTR foam, resin, fiberglass

COLLECTION OF DANIEL THOMSON

"Deathstar" modern planing hull five fin

2009; 59" × 17.25" × 2.25"; XTR foam, resin, carbon fiber

COLLECTION OF DANIEL THOMSON

TOMO/FIREWIRE PRODUCTION CREW, THAILAND,
HANDMADE FINS BY CARL EKSTROM

*Vanguard modern planing hull eco prototype with
foam core and veneer laminate*

2013; 66" × 18.5" × 2.375"; Recycled EPS foam, paulownia,
epoxy seal, bamboo fins

COLLECTION OF MARK PRICE

Plate 88
Epilogue: Branded Production Board Prototype, 2013

The board shown here is a recent example of an industrial craft surfboard. With the exception of the fins (which were handcrafted from bamboo by Carl Ekstrom), this board was built in a factory using a series of mechanized processes. That being said, it was born of handcraftsmanship. The prototype of the design was hand-shaped by Daniel Thomson. The hand shape was then scanned and digitized. This information was programmed into a cutting machine, which cut the blank from recycled foam. The exterior wood pieces were made in a similar fashion.

This board is a modern planing hull; its design is a direct descendant of the boards that Bob Simmons made in the 1940s and 1950s. As discussed earlier in this book, the planing principles used by Simmons are found in the finless surf craft of ancient Hawai'i, so in that sense, this board is con-

the single-fin era and the boards of IPS. The board has five fin boxes and will function with a variety of fin set-ups, including no fin at all. By thoughtfully combining his own thoroughly researched insights into hydrodynamic design with elements from different eras of surfing, Thomson has come close to making a universal high-performance board.

The board's foam core and wood-composite laminate construction can also be traced back to Simmons, whose late 1940s "sandwich" boards layered Styrofoam, marine plywood, balsa, resin, and fiberglass in a similar construction process. The board shown here, however, has no fiberglass or resin on the exterior. It is finished simply with epoxy-sealed sheets of paulownia wood. The end result is a board that is functional, beautiful, light, strong, and very environmentally

friendly, especially when compared to a standard polyurethane board. It is also knowingly and meaningfully connected to ancestral designs.

As an example of industrial craft, this board fulfills many of the ideals expressed by Sōetsu Yanagi in *The Unknown Craftsman.* Here, a reverence for the past inspired Thomson to handcraft his own designs to ride and use. That process in turn led to a production board that is environmentally sustainable, attractive, and well suited for its intended use. It's a board a surfer could be happy with for a long, long time.

Support for this publication and accompanying exhibition is provided in part by the following donors and all the members of Mingei International Museum.

ANCESTORS TO THE FUTURE
Providing for the Museum in their estate plans

Barbara Adachi*
Jane Ahring*
Claire Anderson
Anonymous
Norm Applebaum, AIA
Maurine B. Beinbrink
Angelina Boaz
Robyn Bottomley
Patricia C. Dwinnell Butler*
Mary and J. Dallas Clark*
Kathleen and Joel Cook
Roger C. Cornell, M.D.
Florence B. Covell
Kathryn Crane
Katy and Mike Dessent
Alice and Doug Diamond
DeWitt Drury
James Eisen and Madeleine Kemp-Eisen
John and Fran Ferris
Walter Fitch, III*
Audrey S. Geisel
Mrs. Milton D. Goldberg*
Jean Hahn and John I.* Hardy
Marilee Hong
Nancy and Steve Howard
Frances Hunter
Robert Bruce Inverarity*
Gladys Lucille Johnstone*
Charmaine and Maurice Kaplan*
Louisa S. Kassler*
Maurice Kawashima
Maureen Pecht King
Greg La Chapelle*
Theresa Lai
Clara and L. Curtis* Larson
Charlotte G. and Don B. Leiffer*
Martha Longenecker*
Josephine R. MacConnell
The Mayers Family Trust
Lane and Elaine McVey
Juanita H. Dahlstrom Miller*
Nancy Nenow
Carolyn and Tom Owen-Towle
Gwendolyn Peacher*
Sydney Martin Roth*
Beverly Sheiffer*
Curt Sherman
Rob Sidner

192 |

Nancy E. Snyder
Dorothy Day Stewart*
Leona Mercer Vennard*
Dorothy Vogler
Joanne C. and Frank R. Warren
Bert Waxler
Therese Whitcomb
Thomas A. White
Terri Peterson Zimdars
*deceased

FOUNDER'S CIRCLE
Leading growth of the Museum's collection and permanent endowment

Jean Hahn Hardy, Honorary Chair

Anonymous
Carol and Martin Dickinson
Audrey S. Geisel
Ingrid B. Hibben and Victor La Magna
Maureen and Charles King
Dr. Laurie Mitchell and Brent Woods
Susan and Fred Oliver
Rob Sidner
Hope Turney
Joanne C. and Frank R. Warren

CONNOISSEURS
Dedicated to building the Museum's collection

Jan Bart, Chair

Norman Blachford and Peter Cooper
Sue K. Edwards
Joan and Irwin Jacobs
Maurice M. Kawashima
Barbara G. Kjos
Courtenay McGowen
Christa McReynolds
John and Patricia Seiber
Ron and Mary Taylor
Christy Walton
Frances Hamilton White

CORPORATE, FOUNDATION AND GOVERNMENT SUPPORTERS

Akaloa Resource Foundation
Anne Ray Charitable Trust
Bloomingdale's Fund at the Macy's Foundation
The City of San Diego
The County of San Diego
Design/One Modern

The Donald C. and Elizabeth M. Dickinson Foundation
HSBC
Las Patronas
Lawrance Contemporary Furniture
The Legler Benbough Foundation
Mandell Weiss Charitable Trust
The Margaret A. Cargill Foundation
Maurice J. Masserini Charitable Trust
Mister California
Modern San Diego
Northern Trust
Ortegas Mexican Bistro
The Parker Foundation
Patrons of the Prado

PROGRESS

Qualcomm Foundation
Quilter's Guild of Dallas
Rancho Self Storage
The Thomas C. Ackerman Foundation
UBS Financial Services
Union Bank
U~T San Diego
Waters Fine Catering
Wells Fargo Bank Foundation

THE DIRECTOR'S CIRCLE
Furnishing core support for the Museum's exhibitions

Courtenay McGowen, Chair

Paul and Mindy Aisen
Norm Applebaum, AIA and Barbara Roper
Frances M. Armstrong
Cia and Larry Barron
Darlene Bates
LaDean Berry and Lauren Murphy
April and Lowell Blankfort
Althea Brimm
Gordon Brodfuehrer
Ellen Brown Merewether and Ray Merewether
Rhonda Brown
Joyce Butler
Carmela M. Caldera
Louisa Campagna
Lesley and David Cohn
H. Michael and Jean Collins
Mary E. Collins
Roger C. Cornell, M.D.
Ann Craig
Kathryn Crane
Robert and Elisabeth Crouch
Alison Cummings and Phil Pryde
Nancy N. Danninger

Jim and Mary Dawe
Matthew Dente
Alice and Doug Diamond
Mary Dilligan
Clive and Olivia Dorman
Lorrain and John Duffy
Drs. Steve Eilenberg and Marie Tartar
Heidi and John Farkash
Danah H. Fayman
Joan Fisher
Chris Frahm
Cynthia Furlong
Connie K. Golden
Mr. and Mrs. Michael E. Hallor
Susan Hayes
Richard C. Helmstetter
Thomas and Alison Henry
Lawrence and Suzanne Hess
Ken and Sandy High
Carol F. Hinrichs
Jerry and Linda Hirshberg
Traci Hong
Steve and Nancy Howard
Jay and Mary Jayne Jones
John Ippolito
Gary Jugum
Mr. and Mrs. Frederick Kleinbub
Bonnie Knoke
Ellen Koutsky
Dr. and Mrs. Jay Kovtun
Theresa Lai
Robin J. Lipman
Beverly Maloof
Carol R. Miller
Rena Minisi and Rich Paul
Rebecca and David Mrachek
Ruth Mulvaney
Lyn Nelson
Nancy Nenow
Thomas and Patricia Nickols
Revs. Carolyn and Tom Owen-Towle
Lawrence Paull and Marcy Bolotin
Tom and Karen Pecht
Phil and Pam Reed
John and Dannie Reis
Claire K.T. Reiss
Jan and Doug Rightmer
Dr. and Mrs. Alan Robbins
Thomas and Beatrice Roberts
Mrs. William C. Ruzich
Taal Safdie and Ricardo Rabines
Robert and Lora Sandroni
Kay Sekimachi
Curt Sherman
Virginia and Lawrence Sherwood
John R. Siglow
Jack C. and Bonnie Sipe
Joel and Dotti Sollender
Jeanette Stevens

Bonnie and Ray Stewart
Gwen Stoughton
Dr. Miriam Summ
J.L. Tanzer
The John M. and Sally B. Thornton Foundation
Molly Thornton
Paul and Nel Van Elderen
Viterbi Family Grant Fund of the Jewish Community Foundation
Lili S. and Eugene S. Walsh
Nell Waltz
Mary K. Waters
Mr. and Mrs. Howard Weiner
Dr. Ray Weiss and Abby Silverman Weiss
Mr. and Mrs. Jean-René Westfall
Therese T. Whitcomb
Lana Wilson
Richard Woltman
Carolyn Yorston-Wellcome
Terri Peterson Zimdars

December 5, 2013